Thinklesticks
The Mind Garden

Joanna Louise Wright

DEDICATION

To the woman who always believed in me even when I
didn't believe in myself. The person who supports my
dreams as soon as the idea seed pops into my head. The
woman who makes the best cup of tea in the world.
Thank you Mum.

CONTENTS

ACKNOWLEDGEMENTS

This book has been a massive project. I have been on an incredible journey of discovery. It all started with a blank notebook and a pen. I was doodling in the sunshine one summer's afternoon in 2014, after I finished the first draft of my novel "Benchmark". I realised I had stumbled across a hobby that I loved. Drawing stick people! I blended this with another passion, Personal Development, and Thinklesticks was born.

I would like to say a huge thank you to everyone who has given up their time to be involved in my Mind Garden Research Project. Those 90 minute meetings (often much longer than that…sorry!!) have given me such extraordinary insight into how we interpret our internal experience of life. You are all very much a part of this book. You gave me the confidence and inspiration to drive this project forwards and ultimately create The Mind Garden. You all mean so much to me. Thank you.

Thank you to my amazingly supportive Mum who encouraged me from the very first Doodle. She has a never ending supply of positivity for Thinklesticks and it has helped so much on those difficult days when I've been up to my eyeballs with work, deadlines and software failures. She has seen it all. The good, the bad and the ugly. Thank you Mum for everything.

Thank you to my amazing sons, Harvey and Ronan for their continued support and love. They are now following their own dreams and cultivating lives for themselves at University. I could not be prouder of the young men they have become. Always and forever the Best Boys in the World!

Thank you to my lovely Dad for all the coffee mornings listening to my crazy ideas and convincing me that they are not crazy at all! Your sausage sandwiches are the best. Thank you also to the rest of my family, Graham, Jo, Jack, Ben, Anneke, Alice, Matthew and my extended family for being you.

Thank you also to all the friends I call family. I really am the luckiest girl to have you all by my side through life. Tam, Miss Loraine, Keisha, Miss V, Mary, Kath, Pat, Jen, Adam and the Girls, The Classy Ladies, The Carlo Rossi Army, The Caversham Dining Club, my WiggleWaggle Family, everyone at Wright School of Dance and anyone I've missed out! I must say a special thank you to my Superhero friend Justin Lee for saving me during the Self-Publishing process. You are amazing.

An enormous thank you to my fantastic PA, Claire. She has transformed my working life with her organisation, forward thinking and all round excellence. Running a dance school AND trying to work on this project would not have been possible without her. Thank you for all that you do. I have to say we make a pretty awesome team. Thank you.

Thank you also to my absolute creative genius of a friend Pat Lewis for yet another wonderful front cover and logo design. Thank you also for your belief in Thinklesticks from the start and for your words of encouragement at every stage. Thank you also for introducing me to Matt Rogers who has animated the Thinklesticks logo. Thank you Matt. I love it!

If I can help just one mind to find clarity then it will have been worth all the work. Happy Mind Gardening!

Much love,

Joanna Louise Wright

INTRODUCTION

I have, first hand, experienced life on my default setting. I believed I was a product of circumstance and that life just 'happened' to me. I felt I had experienced a lot of personal struggles and was not where I thought I should be. As far as I was concerned, I'd been dealt a tough hand of cards and played them extremely unwisely.

Life wasn't all bad. There were two aces in my pack; my two children. I had good friends and family who could lift me up most days. I had enough money to afford food, heat, light and the odd pair of shoes. In theory, I should have been happy enough but life felt like an everyday battle and it definitely wasn't fair.

At the age of 30 I was an emotional wreck. I was full to the brim of unhelpful past hurt, disappointment, dashed hopes and dreams, failed relationships, damaging self beliefs, very little confidence or low self esteem.

I seemed to be able to function on the outside; look after my children, go to work, see friends and present as a normal version of me but I allowed all kinds of fears to govern my choices and had found myself stuck in a seemingly endless and unenjoyable rut.

It was at this point that I realised my reactions to certain events, problems, situations and relationships were increasingly irrational. Every problem felt like a massive blow until one day I just couldn't cope anymore.

With tears streaming down my face, unknown to me what the roots of those tears were, I decided to reach out to a counsellor. That moment was one of life's crossroads for me. A very difficult step but probably the most important of my life. I had no clue whether it would help or what help would actually feel like, or indeed, whether I was beyond help but I felt that I had been living in Struggle City for a long time and I was desperate to get out of that desolate place. Even when the sun shone in Struggle City I could not feel the warmth on my skin, due to the constant cloud cover overhead.

HARMFUL: Causing or likely to cause harm.
Synonyms: damaging, detrimental, dangerous, negative,
unhealthy, destructive

Harmful

Helpful

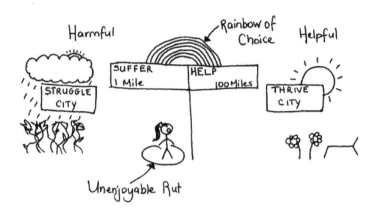

HELPFUL: Useful. Ready to give help.
Synonyms: caring, pleasant, beneficial, positive, practical

I was sitting in the waiting room of the Therapy Centre, nervous, anxious, scared and weak, when I glanced out of the big, old sash window into the garden. It was an entangled mess full of overgrown weeds, dying trees, old junk and long unkempt grass. There were a few beautiful flowers attempting to brighten up the display but they didn't stand much chance against the aggressively tanglesome growth. I suddenly felt drawn to it, as if it signified exactly how my mind felt. I was that garden. A complete mess.

It hadn't been looked after for years and, as a result, it was becoming unmanageable and would need a serious amount of work to get it under control. I would need a serious amount of work to get myself under control.

I felt tears form in my eyes as the heaviness hit me again. I had no energy to do the work needed. Even if I had the energy, where would I find the time? Even if I had the time how would I know where to start? Then I heard the counsellor call my name and I was jolted back to reality. For the first time ever I entered my Mind Garden with the intent of finding a way to manage it.

Ten years later, my Mind Garden is unrecognisable. During that decade I have been actively learning, studying, growing and enhancing my skills as a Mind Gardener. I have developed an innate self awareness through consistent digging, planting, weeding, nourishing and designing on a daily basis.

The benefits of this work are incredible and something I would never have predicted. In the first 30 years of my life I had not stumbled across the term 'Personal Development' or 'Mind Management'. The words 'Self Help' had been bandied about in society but, in truth, it was an alien concept to me. I felt strongly that I couldn't help myself because it wasn't ME causing the damaging situations; it was the damaging situations and toxic people that kept magnetising to me for some unknown reason. I was a good person, but perhaps I had been a bad person in a previous life? Or maybe I was simply unlucky. Unlucky in love, definitely. Unlucky with money, yes. Unlucky in looks? Yep. Although I used the word 'unlucky', with hindsight I can see that I had a 'Powerless' Mindset. Everyone and everything had more power than me and so it felt as if I had little or no control over my circumstances or emotions. It didn't seem to matter how hard I tried, I just continued to attract struggle.

**POWERLESS: Without ability, influence or power.
Synonyms: ineffective, defenceless, vulnerable, helpless, paralysed, incapable, helpless**

**POWERFUL: Having control and influence.
Synonyms: strong, formidable, compelling, effective, impressive, great**

That is until that fateful day in a counselling session when I started to unpick the first roots of an unhelpful weed that was entangling me. I started to use questioning to dig deep and before long I came to the realisation that although there were certain things that were beyond my control, there were also a lot of things that perhaps I could take hold of.

Counselling helped me to reconnect with myself on a deep level (SOIL and FOUNDATIONS). It also helped me to process and accept certain harmful events in my life (WEEDS and BEANSTALKS) so that they did not cause me as much pain. I describe it now as ten months of Garden Clearance; working out what were weeds, why they were there, the effect they were having and then digging them up, with the best of my ability.

In my last counselling session, my counsellor advised me to keep learning about myself, and these words struck a chord with me. I felt I had cleared my garden and now that left me with a very barren setting with just a few nice trees and flowers. It seemed a vast area to fill and a new fear started to appear. What next?

It was then that I stumbled across my first personal development book whilst taking a toilet break at the motorway services. I went to buy a chocolate bar and happened to browse the Best Sellers list. The book's title stood out to me 'How to Be Brilliant' by Michael Heppell. If you have read my first novel 'Benchmark', you will know that the leading lady, Alana Leevy, also followed this path.

The words in that book excited me about taking my life (and my Mind Garden) on as a project. After reading the book I practised many of the suggested exercises and activities and I could instantly feel the benefits of the work I was doing. I then did further reading, 'The Mind Gym', 'The Compound Effect' and many, many more. I would read each book with an open mind and gather up everything I felt that resonated with me, eagerly writing notes, trying to put into my own words the wisdom and insight I had just soaked up.

As I was studying my life and mind, three questions kept popping into my mind:

Why didn't I learn these things in school?

Why have I only just stumbled across this wisdom that is helping me cope with life?

Why are we encouraged to brush our teeth twice daily and yet not encouraged to work on our minds every day?

Those questions made me want to delve deeper into the benefits of Personal Development and Mind Management and so I have spent the last ten years studying in my spare time the works of quality thinkers, mentors, gurus, coaches and inspiring people.

With that passion, alongside the continual creation of my own Mind Garden, I have developed a Doodle World called 'Thinklesticks'. I used to draw these doodles just for me, to enhance my understanding of a concept or analogy and as a quick reference to a deeper topic. I found that in one simple doodle, I could convey a thousand words. Sometimes a thousand words are good. On other days a doodle is all I need.

After I had drawn over 100 doodles I started to wonder whether other people might be able to relate to them, and if so, could they be of help to other internal worlds as they had been to mine.

I decided to investigate and set up a Research Project focusing on The Mind Garden analogy. It is safe to say that I never want the project to end. The questionnaire has confirmed to me that life can be hugely affected by our internal worlds, and when they are not intentionally managed, we are often experiencing life on our default setting. In Mind Garden terms this is like leaving the garden to its own devices. Perhaps it will grow into a beautiful, wild garden (if you're lucky) but if you are unlucky (as I was) the garden will wrap you up in thorny knots until you reach a point where you can hardly breathe.

There are also those gardens where nothing much grows at all, just a bare outlook. This can feel as bad as a weed infestation.

The Thinklesticks Mind Garden is ever evolving but I want to pass on all that has been helpful to me so far, because it has transformed my experience of life. I cannot claim the Mind Garden analogy as my own as it has been used in literature, religion, art and philosophy for thousands of years. I've just taken it and made it work for me. If it works for you too I will be a very happy human.

Joanna Louise Wright

1. GARDEN EMPLOYMENT

In this chapter I will attempt to explain my rather complex idea of Garden Employment. It has taken me a decade to understand myself with journals, experiments, reading, quality thinking and eventually making sense of it all by creating the MIND GARDEN. I am hoping that I can now speed up the process for other people to understand themselves. Awareness is the first step to improvement. I cannot do the hard graft for people, but perhaps the work I have done on myself can help inspire others to experience their internal worlds in much happier ways.

So what is GARDEN EMPLOYMENT? I have assigned titles to the different roles I play within my mind and life. Just as you have a different responsibility as a mum, daughter, friend, colleague or dad, son, brother if you are a male, we have the ability to perform different functions within ourselves when we become aware of them.

The GARDEN EMPLOYMENT TEAM:
Worker, Manager, Designer, Greenhouse Specialist
Lawn Specialist

Worker   Manager   Designer

Lawn Specialist   Greenhouse Specialist

It has been a fascinating area of the Mind Garden interviews. I have seen people realise that they don't have a GARDEN MANAGER or their GARDEN DESIGNER has been on a permanent holiday for the last decade, or their WORKER is exhausted or they don't have a GREENHOUSE SPECIALIST to look after their goals. The concepts seemed to resonate with people far more than I had imagined.

I will attempt to explain how I discovered and developed my Team over time and how they now work so exceptionally well together. I call them my Dream Team.

TEAM: A group of players forming one side in a game or sport. Come together as a team to achieve a common goal.
Synonyms: squad, company, crew, working party join forces, collaborate, work together, unite, integrate

WORKER

WORKER: A person who works, a person who achieves a specific thing. Activity involving mental or physical effort done in order to achieve a result. Synonyms: labour, toil, exertion, effort

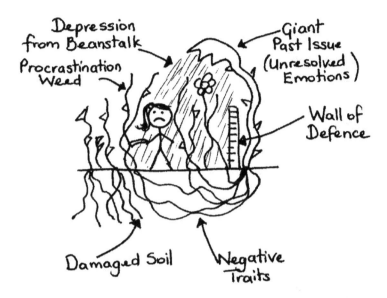

In 2007, Little Worker Joanna had been left to deal with the Mind Garden all by herself. Every so often a very harsh and judgmental boss would march in, take a look around and negatively berate her for being a waste of space, a letdown and list all of her negative traits. She reminded her that the mind garden was a mess and it was all her fault. Little Worker Joanna was downtrodden, tired, heavy and overwhelmed by the jumbled mess. She wanted to make things better but where would she start? She'd make a concerted effort to sort out some practical changes but bad habits had formed. Putting things off, procrastination, laziness and low self esteem made it difficult to see an end to the ever growing

PROBLEM PLANTS, WEEDS and BEANSTALKS. Little Worker Joanna couldn't help but look on the negative side of life because there was not much light in the mass overgrowth. Everyone else's gardens looked so much more attractive than hers. She wished on many occasions that she could swap personalities. She didn't like herself. Other people seemed to like her, which she didn't really understand, but they weren't living in her head.

DEMORALISED: Cause someone to lose confidence or hope.
Synonyms: dishearten, depress, discourage, subdue, weaken

The first serious relationship I had was from the ages of 17-21. It had damaged my SELF SOIL in so many ways. If I tried to plant anything positive in the SOIL it would almost always fail to grow. Or if it grew, I would never be able to feel the real joy of it because it would be entangled within the ever present WEEDS. This led to me feeling a broad sense of demoralisation in many areas. Across my whole LAWN OF LIFE.

With that lingering feeling and the random attacks of an unsympathetic and judgmental MANAGER, who stormed in every so often to criticise, it was no wonder that I was not motivated to make the changes needed. There were no dreams or guidelines to follow. Little Worker Joanna was just constantly chopping down the relentless weeds just to maintain everyday life.

DISAPPOINTMENT: Sadness or displeasure caused by the non-fulfilment of one's hopes or expectations. Synonyms: sadness, regret, dismay, sorrow, heavy-heartedness, depression, disillusionment, discontent, dissatisfaction

I was a good Mum. A devoted single parent. I knew I put my heart and soul into my children and I was proud of that. On a personal level though, I often felt that I was not where I thought I should be. I had failed at marriage and numerous other relationships. I hadn't done well in my A-Levels and I hadn't gone to University. I had friends who I treasured but I often felt that I was putting on a front. If they really knew what a mess I was inside they wouldn't want to be around me. Regret scratched me like thorns. "If only I'd been stronger…", "If only I'd done things differently…", "If only I had more confidence…". If only. At the age of 30 Little Worker Joanna had sunk into depression…

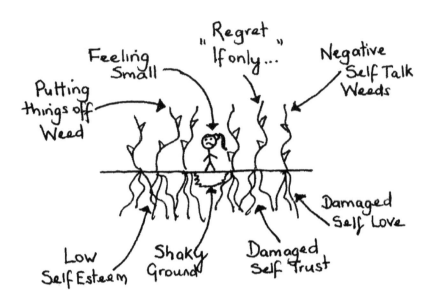

"It's just one thing after another…"

It seemed like a series of difficult events had ruined my garden and at that point when I crumbled and went to see my counsellor for the first time, it had seemed so overwhelmingly difficult to do anything about it. My emotions were battered and bruised from trying to get back up and sort things out to then turn around and be confronted with yet another problem. Little had I realised at the time that so many of the DISASTERS had been handmade. Some had been a little harder to control but the damaged soil really was creating most of the issues that were ongoing.

I was better able to be a good gardener for my children. I helped them out, I looked after them, and I tended to their gardens far more than I tended to mine. That is natural as a parent and I used to say "As long as my boys are happy, that's all that matters." I would invest my energy and time into them and I loved to do that, but I neglected my own garden. I avoided my own garden as much as possible. Eventually I realised that the neglect was having an adverse effect on how much I could give to my boys. They barely noticed it but I just didn't have the same drive or determination. I wasn't, in any way, showing them a strong, positive example on how to live a happy life. I was just going through the motions. I never lost my ability to look after my children's needs but I did lose the ability to inspire them, for a while. It was one of the main reasons why I decided to take myself on. I wanted them to know that there was a better way to live. I wanted to set a good example.

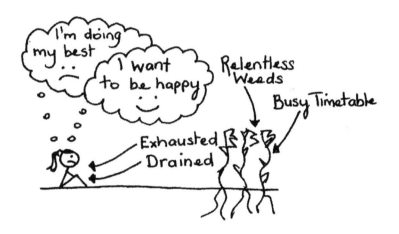

At the end of each day I would feel drained.

DRAINED: Cause to be lost or used up.
Synonyms: exhausted, depleted, expended, emptied,
sapped, strained.

I would give of myself to my children, to my job and to my friends and family but, by the end of the day, I would have nothing left to give to myself and so would find that all I could do was zombie in front of the TV. I'd get up the next day and repeat the cycle. For 10 years. Then I crashed and burned. My SOIL had dried up due to lack of nourishment. The WEEDS were out of control due to lack of care and attention. The BEANSTALKS had grown so large that they were unmanageable. That was until I read two very important books which I will explain in the MANAGER section. If I hadn't read those books I believe wholeheartedly that I would still be in that habitual cycle of giving and exhaustion. I was constantly in other people's gardens doing work for them, probably, if I'm honest, to avoid doing any work in my own jumbled garden. Then at the end of the day I had a good excuse to not be focusing on myself. After all I was such a nice person giving to everyone else the whole time. I was selfless. It didn't matter about Little Worker Joanna's well being as long as everyone else was ok. That was until Little Worker Joanna had nothing left to give.

BREAKDOWN: A failure of a relationship or system.
Synonyms: collapse, disintegration, failure

I want to make it clear that I had a supportive network of people around me. I was not alone in my daily life. People cared deeply about me. My breakdown was entirely internal. No one could have known what was going on inside me. I believe that my inability to cope was completely down to the fact that my inner GARDEN EMPLOYMENT system had failed. The Team had deserted Little Worker Joanna many,

many years ago and actually in some cases they had never even been employed. Was it any wonder that the one little worker had reached her limits? She'd done her best. She'd fought on. She'd tried to be as strong as she could be but it was just too much to ask of anyone.

That phone call to the counsellor, I believe, was the first job of the garden MANAGER. She'd finally stepped in and said:

"Help is needed."

I will go into further detail about how the counselling sessions helped Little Worker Joanna in the section on WEEDS and BEANSTALKS. It assisted dramatically to tackle the bigger issues that had been so difficult to deal with. A lot of weeding took place which had led to a calmer mind, more able to deal with everyday life again. However, no big changes had taken place. The everyday hectic lifestyle continued taking its toll on the garden in its own way.

It was then, in 2008, that I started to read self development books and my garden MANAGER was employed.

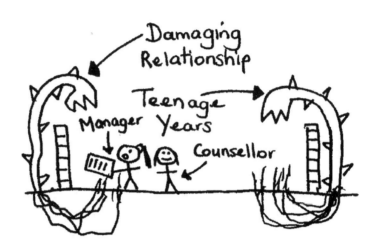

MANAGER

MANAGER: A person responsible for controlling or administering an organisation of group of staff. A person in charge of the activities, tactics and training of a team. A person regarded in terms of their skill in managing resources.
Synonyms: organiser, controller, leader, boss

The first project my MANAGER took on was TIME. Life Changer.

'Good time management skills - you'll feel the freedom from deadline pressure and stress in general. You'll be more productive, procrastinate less and have more time to relax which further helps decrease stress and anxiety." - Google.

People have started to ask me, "How do you have the time to do everything you do?" Often it's a rhetorical question, a remark of passing wonder and very rarely are they looking for the actual answer. However, I am always eager to share how I have the time for everything that I do because 'Time Management' was one of the first skills I worked on in my development journey.

I used to say:

"I don't have time to write a book."

"I don't know where the time goes, it's Friday again and I was going to do so much this week."

"I'm exhausted and I still didn't get much ticked off my to do list."

"I just don't have the time."

Time was always getting away from me. I was a slave to my busy, hectic, rush-around single parent life which, at the end of the day, I would feel so worn out by that I would have to zombie on the sofa for some well=deserved down time in front of the TV, to relax. Ironically, the programmes I sat down in front of rarely had a relaxing effect on me but I did an exceptional job of convincing myself that they did. Escapism was also a factor.

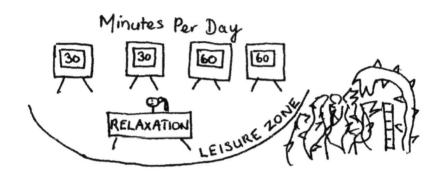

It was certainly a rut and one that I had been in for years. Running around after my children's social and sporting lives, saying 'yes' to things, even when I wasn't too keen to do them (it would be rude not to), fitting in work around school times, cooking dinner, chores, keeping up with friends, attempting romance and anything and everything else that life brought along. I was reacting to life on a daily basis without any thought of how time slips away and how habits add up. Until one day I read a paragraph which really made me think:

"If you watch 2 to 3 hours of TV a day then don't tell me you haven't got time to achieve your goals."

Mmm. It was an uncomfortable slap in the face. At first a slight denial - "Well the person in this book obviously has no idea how exhausting my days are - they'd need to watch TV and relax if they were me." But the words stuck in my head, as they so often did. Two or three hours a day. I was probably guilty of that. Guilty. Guilty of saying "I don't have time." Mmm. I was probably guilty of four hours on a Sunday as I liked that morning kitchen show it made me smile. Downton Abbey, I couldn't miss. I'd also often be zombie-fied in front of the end of Songs of Praise, Antiques Roadshow (which I consistently moaned about) and a re-run of an American Teen Show with my boys. Dammit. The man was right.

As an experiment I decided to monitor my TV time. Well… I wish I hadn't looked.

30   Mins Breakfast TV
30   Mins Neighbours
1   Hour of Soap Operas
1   Hour News/Local News

Pretty much every…single…day. Apart from Saturdays and Sundays when in the evenings, I clocked up 4 hours of a concoction of X-Factor, Lottery Programmes, Harry Hill and You've Been Framed. You've Been Framed - embarrassing moments in people's lives. I was experiencing my own embarrassing moment…

23 Hours of TV a week, practically every week, probably for the last ten years. Oh.

I had recently finished reading yet another fantastic book 'The Compound Effect' by Darren Hardy. This focused on habits adding up over time. 'How to be Brilliant' and 'The Compound Effect' collided in my mind and I did the sums.

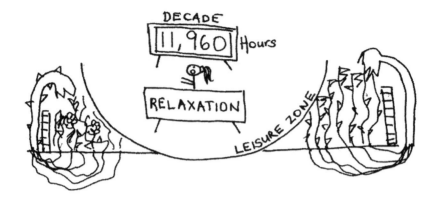

3   Hours a day (approx but more on weekends)
23   Hours a week
92   Hours in a month (GULP)

Slightly scared to calculate the rest.

598   Hours in 6 months
1196 Hours in a year

Oh my…

2392 Hours in 2 years.
No way.
I stopped to recalculate as this couldn't be right.

5890 Hours in 5 years.
11960 Hours in 10 years.

No way.
I checked the sums ten times.
The results stayed the same.

I remember slamming my notebook down and wondering why on earth I was doing this to myself. I thought Personal Development was supposed to make you feel better? Self awareness was a good thing. Really? At that moment it felt the opposite. Negative emotions were creeping in - embarrassment, guilt, confusion - I can't have watched TV for 11,960 hours of my life over the last ten years? That was just a crazy number. It was only three hours a day. Bits of programmes here and there, to relax me from my busy, stressful, rush-around days. The news to keep me informed, a little bit of entertainment to add some happiness. I mean, I didn't go out much, I didn't smoke, I was a hardworking single Mum, I deserved those hours didn't I? I mean it's not as if I was doing anything wrong. So why was I feeling so awkward and uncomfortable?

I suddenly felt quite bitter about the data I'd collected. It had put me in a bad mood. I left the task and went to watch the X-Factor Final, an extended episode, to help me with my escapism from my mood. Damn. I was now aware that I was watching it to distract myself from life. I now knew that a 2 hour programme watched once a week was 8 hours, over a year was 96 hours. Mmm. You cannot unlearn an incredible fact like that. You can try to ignore it but you can't forget it.

There is a process for me in Personal Development. It's not all easy. Far from it. My effectiveness, positivity, wisdom, joy and love for what I do has arisen from huge internal struggles along the way. No one was with me in the garden when I realised that I had no GARDEN MANAGER. I had no self-managing skills, no time management skills and I felt ashamed. Looking inside myself with clarity was a hard wake up call. The only employer I had was a single WORKER, constantly trying to fight the WEEDS, BEANSTALKS and entangled flowers. She worked so hard that at the end of the day all she could do was sit and watch TV.

"I had no time to write a book."

Mmm… well that was a big fat lie. I actually had 11960 hours in a decade to write a book. Ouch. I had 11960 hours to sort my life out.

After the initial negativity, I slowly but surely started to think more neutrally. Wow. 11960 hours was a lot. If I wasn't watching TV - could I use that time to write a book/retrain professionally/feel better about myself? What could I do with all that time?

I didn't immediately take action on this new revelation. I slowly pondered on the information. Days went by and a strange feeling of unrest set upon me whenever I was watching TV. The innocence had been spoiled, a new light was shining on the situation and my mind became distracted by thoughts of all those hours. The possibilities. Yet, was I ready for that? Was I ready to discard the comfort of my routine and replace it with…what? Surely you could do a lot of things in 23 hours a week. I worked 30 hours a week and was a devoted parent, but I still managed to habitually watch 23 hours of TV a week.

In the same period of time I read an article in my new magazine subscription 'Psychologies'. A whole dossier section on making your dreams come true. It was advising setting aside 30 minutes a day on a dream you want to achieve and how little and often could be a very successful way of achieving goals which you've had sitting on your list for ages. All the information was syncing together in my mind.

EXCITEMENT: A feeling of great enthusiasm and eagerness
Synonyms: exhilaration, elation, anticipation, zest, spark, adventure, buzz

I questioned whether I had been managing myself at all up until then. I concluded that I would get dragged along by life for about 6 months at a time until I felt quite overwhelmed by everything and then a harsh, judgemental boss came along and said:

"Well this is all a big mess. What are you going to do about it?"

Then there would be some concerted effort to make improvements but they were often surface and never long lasting. This would then be repeated every 6 months leading to a vicious cycle which seemed to get worse every time.

The benefits of sitting down and studying time management were immense. In the past, I had only ever considered that my work hours were my structure for the week and that life would somehow have to slot around that. The data from my TV Experiment changed that, thankfully.

The Value of Time
My Awake Hours - 7-11pm (approx) 16 Hours a day

16	Hours in a day
112	Hours in a week
485	Hours in a month
2912	Hours in 6 months
5824	Hours in a year
11648	Hours in 2 years
29120	Hours in 5 years
58240	Hours in 10 years

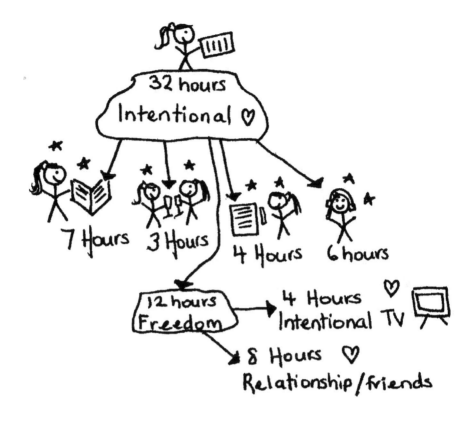

Growth Laboratory Experiment:
Trial out Intentional Time

INTENTIONAL: Done on purpose, deliberate.
Synonyms: planned, conscious, purposeful

I concluded that my GARDEN MANAGER would be responsible for managing 112 hours a week. 112! Daunting? Yes. Exciting? Yes.

I decided to start small not too drastic a change. I had read that although making massive changes can be very effective, often subtle changes were easier to cope with. That seemed to work for me.

My GARDEN MANAGER decided to stop watching 'Neighbours' (30 mins) and deliberately turn the TV off at that time and get a notebook, or a Personal Development book. It was 'Positive Change Time'.

I cannot tell you how powerful the change was. I was deliberately choosing to turn off the TV (powerful) and actively using that time to take a positive step towards something I'd always said I didn't have time for. Now I did have time. I had MADE time. I had taken control of something I had said I didn't have control over and reclaimed it for myself.

It was a tiny change which had massive knock-on effects. I continued this experiment from Monday-Friday and wrote a whole chapter of a story. By Friday, I was not even thinking about the plot of Neighbours I was missing out on. I had felt pangs of need Mon-Thurs to find out if Karl Kennedy was out of hospital but by Friday I presumed he would be and the desire to know had left me.

Instead, I was excited by the things I had read and written. I decided, in MANAGER Mode, to continue the experiment Mon-Fri the following week. By the time 4 weeks had passed, I had clocked up 10 Intentional Hours of writing instead of Neighbours.

When I explained to family and friends about the experiment the reaction was mixed:

"But you love Neighbours, you deserve that time out."

"Good for you!"

"Well I'm not giving it up!"

I think people thought it was a bit odd. Until the results started showing years later.

I enjoyed my 30 minutes a day so much that I started to wonder whether I'd miss the News at Ten. It was something I'd always watched even through my teen years, to keep up to date with what was happening in the world. Never ever cheerful, but it seemed a necessary thing. What if I reclaimed that time for my life too? In the second month I decided to trial it and use the time to read and write.

Growth Laboratory Experiment:
Reclaiming TV time for Dreams

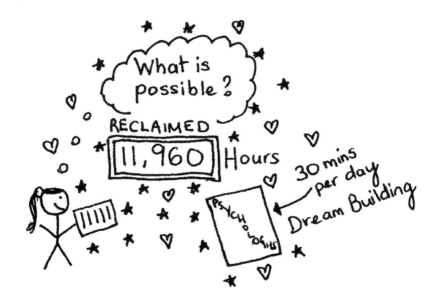

Ever so slowly, I could see the words adding up in my notebook. It really was slow. I'm not going to lie. I had no idea how to write a novel. I hadn't written properly since I was at school, apart from journaling. Yet each 100 words I reached felt like a massive win.

Those two simple changes, those two time tweaks gave me the freedom to start pursuing the things my Garden DESIGNER had tentatively envisioned. She had been missing for years. For the first time ever my Garden MANAGER and DESIGNER were intentionally working together and it felt incredible. I had made progress already and I was gaining momentum. The positive emotions were hard to ignore; pride, excitement and belief, all of which enriched my soil in so many ways.

The Growth Laboratory Experiment was working. My dream of writing a book had been taken from the seed packet chosen by the DESIGNER and given to the MANAGER. She had created a space in the life timetable to plant it. The WORKER had been disciplined to get the writing done in the allocated times. The result... a little seedling of a dream was starting to grow and come to life. Only then did I realise I needed a GREENHOUSE and a GREENHOUSE SPECIALIST. This little seedling needed nurturing. It felt special. I will go into more detail about the discovery of the DESIGNER and the GREENHOUSE SPECIALIST a little later in the chapter.

In the same year that I discovered the benefits of Time Management, I also studied Situation Management, another skill for my newly employed MANAGER to take control of.

RESILIENCE: Ability to withstand or recover quickly from difficult conditions.
Synonyms: strong, tough, buoyant, irrepressible, adaptable, flexible, difficult to keep down

When I first studied Situation Management it was an alien concept to me. I used to have a LOT of problems, one after the other, in fact. It never rained but it poured and if I was lucky enough to have a few problem free days, it wouldn't be long before a hurricane hit. I was never without some sort of problem to deal with, dragging me down, making me feel like I needed to escape from life for a few hours.

I can't remember where I first read about it but when I did it was a revelation to me. It was not a quick fix but with practise and persistence Situation Management has helped enormously in getting my Mind Garden to flourish.

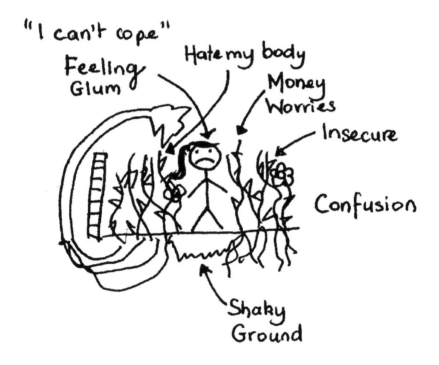

When I was not managing my mind or myself, all problems felt massive. I had not learned key skills in resilience - I had been weakened by circumstances and damaging relationships so I felt I always had to turn to others for advice and support. Also, I had many unsupportive habits which caused extra self-made problems; laziness, procrastination, indifference, lack of confidence, putting things off, bad money management, negativity, disorganisation, overwhelm and overthinking, jealousy, comparisons, pessimism - the list is long!

The benefit of working on my Self Awareness was that I had learnt that I could step away from my problems and start to 'assess' them.

ASSESS: Evaluate or estimate the nature, ability or quality of.
Synonyms: evaluate, judge, rate, analyse, determine

From the Latin word assidere - to sit by

It is such a powerful exercise "to sit" with your problems and assess them. To press the pause button, get a pen and a piece of paper and write down everything that is looping around your head and ask the question:
"What's making me feel irritated, overwhelmed, stressed, anxious, disturbed, depressed, down, blue or whatever emotion is winning out on the day?"
I really had never done this. Such a simple task, it seemed inconceivable that I hadn't taken this common sense approach to problems before, but as I became aware quite quickly in my Personal Development journey, 'common sense' was very rarely commonly used! Not by me anyway!
I had heard in a speech by Jim Rohn that you need to grow to the size of your problems. Mmm. Grow? Not

possible. I was 5′ 3″ and no growth had taken place since I was 15. Growth was not a word that resonated with me. For years I read it without associating myself with it. How can you grow? But slowly the concept started to make sense. Grow in confidence, grow in resilience, grow in knowledge. Growth, as a human. When I'd first listened to those words "grow to the size of the problems", I was put off by that. I didn't understand. But as I did the work, made the notes, did the analysis, the assessing, the problem solving, the experiments, I realised I was growing. Growing in strength, resilience and self-awareness.

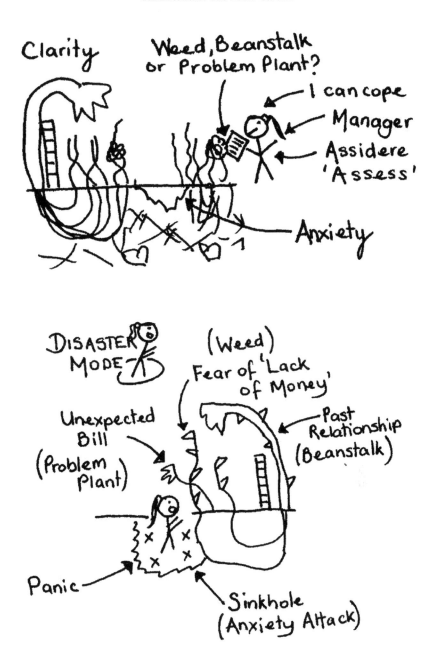

When you sit by your problems, at first they may seem like a disaster - especially if there are high emotions involved. There may be no clear solution. However, it is hard to see one in DISASTER MODE. It is likely that you are on high alert, hypersensitive, fighting fires, panicking and not making great decisions.

So when a problem arises I try to establish what MODE I'm in. At first it's usually one of the NEGATIVE modes.

DISASTER MODE
High emotion/high stress/panic

PROBLEM MODE
Moderate stress/constant worry

IRRITATION MODE
Frustration/recurring thoughts/lingering concern

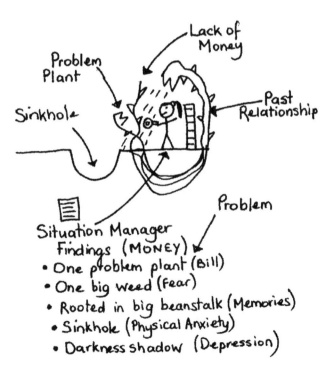

It is then my job to establish what the actual problem is.

Identifying it is not always easy, but it is essential to put it into words, so that I can enter SITUATION MODE.

This requires use of the higher faculties of the mind. PERCEPTION and REASON. How you perceive something is important. Knowing how you perceive something is even more important. Different people see problems in various ways, depending on their perception. I was oblivious to this until I studied the higher faculties of the mind but now it makes so much sense.

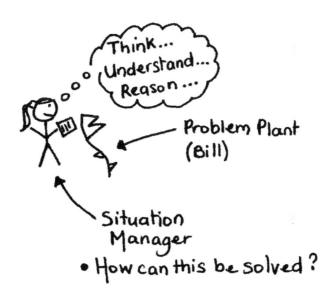

PERCEPTION: The way in which something is regarded, understood or interpreted.
Synonyms: insight, understanding, clarity, intuition, cleverness, intelligence
REASON: The power of the mind to think, understand and form judgments logically.
Synonyms: rationality, logic, reasoning, thought, intellect

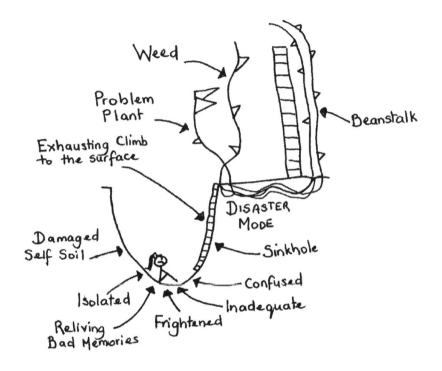

DISASTER: An event or fact which has unfortunate consequences.
Synonyms: catastrophe, failure, shock, adversity, difficulty, heavy blow, fiasco, mess

Emotions are high in DISASTER mode. In fact, sometimes they can lead to panic or anxiety attacks. I cover this more on a personal level in the BEANSTALK chapter. If you enter a situation with a DISASTER mindset it can be very distressing, as you can rarely see a solution. This can be frightening and trigger off all sorts of unwanted feelings. The PROBLEM PLANT can feel enormous and unless you have the skills to quickly assess the reality of the situation (if this really is a disaster or whether it is your mind convincing you it is), it can be a very draining experience to worry about a problem in this mode.

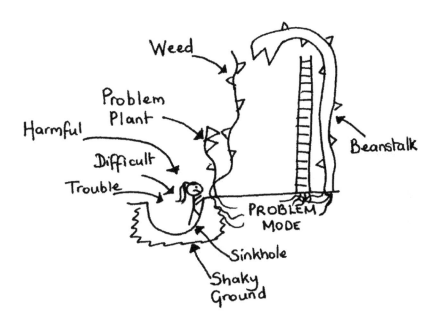

PROBLEM: A matter or situation regarded as unwelcome or harmful and needing to be dealt with and overcome.
Synonyms: difficult, trouble, mess, setback, hassle

Situations in PROBLEM MODE still feel very heavy. Emotions are a struggle. They are not as extreme as in DISASTER MODE but it can still weigh heavily and have a negative effect on life. In PROBLEM MODE solutions are still difficult to find because emphasis is put on the negative outcomes of the situation. It is more likely that a pessimistic approach will win out and a depression could set in. The more PROBLEMS there are in this mode, the more overwhelming things seem to be. Sadness, intense worry, stress, low level anxiety and fear are all evident in PROBLEM MODE. Anger and resentment could also be associated with PROBLEM MODE if it is felt that someone else has planted this problem into your garden.

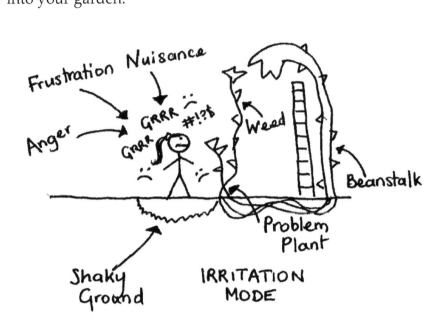

IRRITATION: The state of feeling annoyed, impatient or slightly angry.
Synonyms: annoyance, impatience, vexation, displeasure, nuisance

Irritations are low level problems but they can still have such a negative effect on life enjoyment, especially if they are left unchecked, unmanaged and keep cropping up again and again. They can cause mild anger, grumpiness and general negativity looping round and round. If you are dealing with a situation in IRRITATION MODE it is probable that there is some resentment lingering and it is far less likely that a positive conclusion will be reached. A knee-jerk reactive attitude to an irritation is common, which can escalate the situation to a real problem and even a disaster. IRRITATION MODE is not helpful. It may seem less harmful than DISASTER and PROBLEM MODE but it can be just as damaging long term.

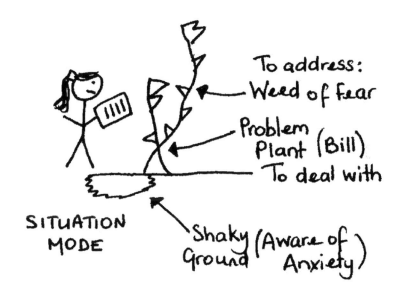

SITUATION: A set of circumstances one finds oneself in.
Synonyms: circumstances, state of affairs, position

SITUATION MODE is quite tricky to reach if you are in one of the negative modes...DISASTER, PROBLEM or IRRITATION. Trying to remove yourself from the entangled emotions of something is a skill that is worth persevering with. I was not innately built with that ability. I was always a worrier. I would have erred on the side of caution and negativity in any situation, especially internally. However, I have proved that SITUATION MANAGEMENT is a skill that can be learned. Once learned, it can be developed. Once developed, it can change your life and your garden for the better. So SITUATION MODE is a NEUTRAL STATE. It is the facts. Not the emotionally swayed interpretation. The facts. The actual situation without the human attachment to it.

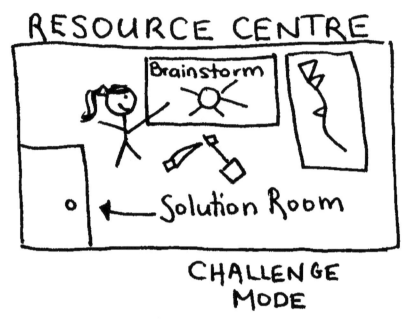

CHALLENGE MODE

**CHALLENGE: A task or situation that tests
someone's abilities.
Synonyms: task, test, obstacle**

I quite like CHALLENGE MODE. The Mindset is a definite shift to the POSITIVE. It is as if you have decided to take on the situation, whatever it is, with a winning mentality. It doesn't mean it will be easy. In fact, the words task, test and obstacle suggest that there will be struggles to overcome. You might have to increase your skills in an area to learn how to pass the test. You might have to research how people have successfully dealt with situations in the past and take on those habits. You might have to ask for the support of your network because the challenge is quite big. But if you can get yourself into CHALLENGE MODE, positive emotions will often drive you forward if you have a clear plan and support from your INTERNAL TEAM. CHALLENGE MODE requires a plan and it requires action.

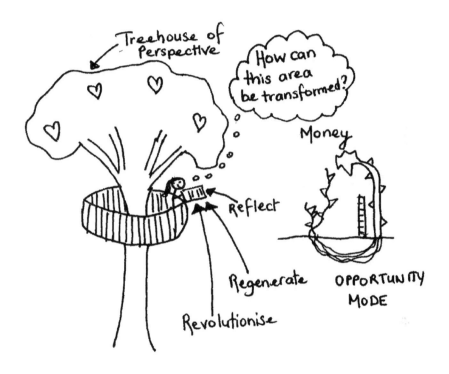

OPPORTUNITY: A favourable, appropriate, or advantageous combination of circumstances. A chance or prospect.
Synonyms: chance, good time, suitable moment, window of opportunity

OPPORTUNITY MODE is my absolute favourite. In fact, now that I've studied the benefits of flipping your problems into opportunities, I try as often as possible to get myself into this mode. OPPORTUNITY MODE requires a vivid and active imagination, strategy, an open mind, good communication skills and a positive mental attitude. It still requires the hard work involved in CHALLENGE MODE and time and energy is needed for researching and planning. There are risks involved because an OPPORTUNITY is not necessarily going to provide the outcome you want but it is the MODE of HOPE, EXCITEMENT, GROWTH and PROGRESS. It is not just about the current situation. It assesses the bigger picture of the garden and looks at how things could change longer term to improve circumstances and pro-actively puts things in place to prevent or at least discourage the same situation returning.

DISASTER, PROBLEM, IRRITATION, SITUATION, CHALLENGE, OPPORTUNITY.

MODES for me are MINDSETS.

I can talk myself into any of them. DISASTER, PROBLEM and IRRITATION are default, knee-jerk mindsets but the quicker I sit with the problems and assess them, the better I'm able to manage them. I call them my PROBLEM PLANTS and my GROWTH CHART. They help to establish whether I'm up for the job or if I need to ask for help. In life, confidence can drop after any event or relationship breakdown, so monitoring how you are feeling is important. Establishing which MODE you are in can really help with Self Awareness. If you realise you are prone to a particular mode and it's not helpful, then perhaps it highlights that work needs to be done in that area.

Problems used to grow freely, regularly and irritatingly in my garden. A combination of weeds, beanstalks and problem plants used to entangle me. I could not differentiate between a problem, weed or beanstalk - they all just caused my life to be difficult.

That is until I created the Problem Plant and Growth Chart Thinklesticks.

A great benefit of becoming an effective Situation Manager is the increase in Self Belief and Self Assurance. When you can sit by your problems from an analytical point of view - from a top management position - there is an overwhelming sense of belief that you can figure things out. Whether it's a Level 1 Annoyance or a Level 10 Serious Issue - if you develop the calm wisdom to sit back and sit by, to assess from a clear thinking position, the outcomes are usually far better and the experience of the situation is improved dramatically, rather than if it was allowed to be dealt with on the default setting.

In garden terms, it's like having the top experts in to see what can be salvaged and what needs to happen to bring about the best outcome. But to be an expert, you must study, and study I did.

I had already established my mind as a garden analogy when I first listened to a speech by Jim Rohn. I had read his name in several Personal Development books. He seemed to be well respected in the area of growth so I looked him up and found numerous YouTube videos of his inspiring talks. I remember the first one I clicked on was an hour long. I watched it late at night and recall being completely captivated by this wise, warm and clever man. His words, it seemed every one of them, spoke to me, as if he understood the exact struggles I had with myself. He did understand because he himself had walked the path of a 'worrier'. I would certainly have called myself an 'overthinker' throughout the first 30 years of my life and as I mentioned before, I could wrap myself in knots for days, weeks or even months.

One particular part of the speech resonated with me so much that I do believe those 41 words guided and encouraged me to dedicate more time to sorting out my untidy garden. Here are the 41 words:

"Weeds come if not controlled, fear gets the upper hand and doubt moves in but managed, worked, given human action with will and knowledge and purpose, and gardens overcome weeds, faith overcomes doubt, and confidence pushed worry into a small place." Jim Rohn.

Those 41 words were quickly followed by these inspirational 13:

"Humans are remarkable. Develop a plan for your life. Create your own environment." Jim Rohn.

Jim Rohn passed away in 2009 and I only discovered him in 2011. Legacy is an incredible thing.

LEGACY: Something left or handed down by a predecessor.
Synonyms: consequence, effect, outcome

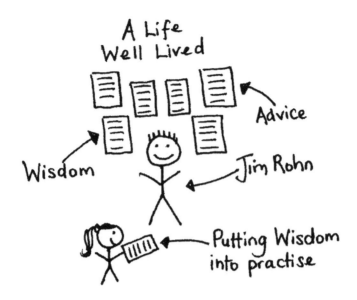

He has left his words with us and if you ever feel that life is getting you down, Google him. I feel like he is the wise grandfather I never had. His words ring in my ears and his wisdom weaves itself into my happiness every day. His most used quote:

"Never wish things were easier, wish you were better." Jim Rohn.

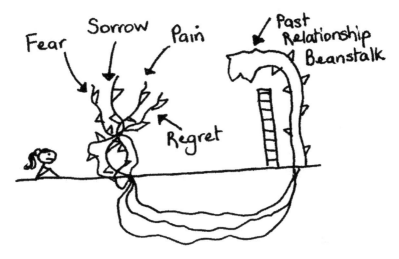

One of his speeches focuses on the damage of worry.

"Worry is the killer of dreams, energy and vitality." - Jim Rohn

WORRY: Feel or cause to feel anxious or troubled about actual or potential problems.

Synonyms: fret, worried, concerned, anxious, agonise, brood, dwell on, panic, get worked up.

Perhaps that was why I was so tired back in the darker days when problems weren't being managed. Another description he used was:

"Fear left unchecked is like a mad dog loose in the house. Sorrow, pain and regret are too high a price to pay not to do something about it." - Jim Rohn.

Pain. I knew all about that. Sorrow was a common emotion. Regrets - I had quite a collection building and I was only 34 at the time.

It is one thing to listen to the words of wisdom of one who has conquered himself and his worry problems and be inspired by him but it is another thing to work out how to take that inspired feeling and know what to do with it. Feeling inspired to make changes is an uplifting state of mind, it brings with it positive vibes of hope and possibility. I would feel instantly motivated to make changes but I still had no clear plan. I now knew that endless worry was not good for me, that confidence would crush fears, that I had to grow my character to be able to cope better but how on earth do you actually do it? How do you go from Level 1 Resilience to Level 10? When you get there, how do you stay there? This is when I started to develop the PROBLEM PLANTS and GROWTH CHART Thinklesticks Tools.

GROWTH LABORATORY EXPERIMENT
Grow to the size of your problems

STEP 1: SELF AWARENESS

Started writing down a list of problems from my head to paper rather than allowing them to fester, brew, expand, enlarge, entangle and explode in my mind.

PROBLEM PLANTS/
WEEDS

STEP 2: ASSESS

Learned how to "Assess" the problems and number them **on a** scale from 1 to 10 on the Problem Plant Scale.

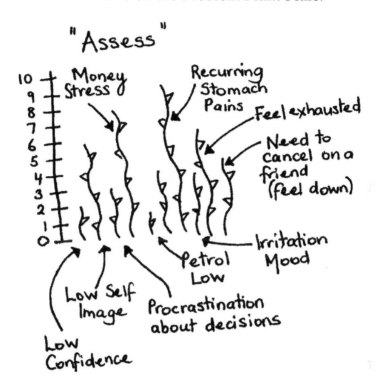

STEP 3: GROWTH CHART

Worked out how big I felt on the Personal Growth Chart in comparison to the problems.

STEP 4: GROWTH LABORATORY SOIL ANALYSIS

Analysed SOIL in Growth Laboratory to discover areas of weakness and struggle which hindered how I felt on the Growth Chart. Highlighted that I was struggling with Self

Confidence, Self Trust, Self Assurance, Self Discipline and most areas of my soil needed attention.

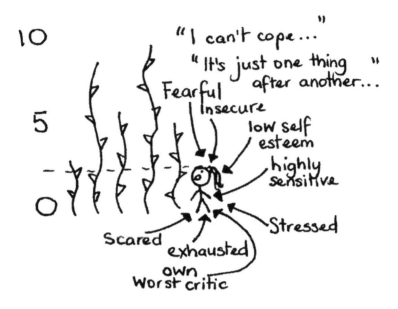

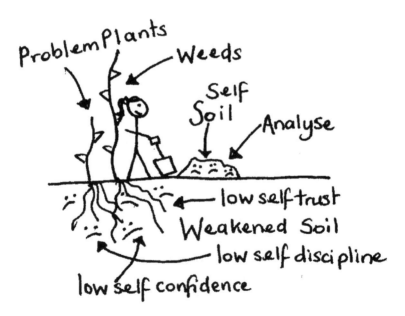

STEP 5: GROWTH PLAN

Created a 6 month Growth Plan to study three main areas of weakness: **Confidence, Self Esteem, Resilience**

STEP 6: COMPLETED PLAN

Read books, listened to audiobooks in the car, watched You Tube videos, Growth Laboratory Experiements.

STEP 7: PROBLEM MODE SYSTEM

Created the Problem Mode System from various wisdom collated and implemented it for all Problem Plants.

STEP 8: WEEKLY PROBLEM SLOT

Established a weekly slot in my timetable to 'Assess' Problem Plants and try to take either a CHALLENGE or OPPORTUNITY viewpoint and develop an action plan to tackle as many as possible.

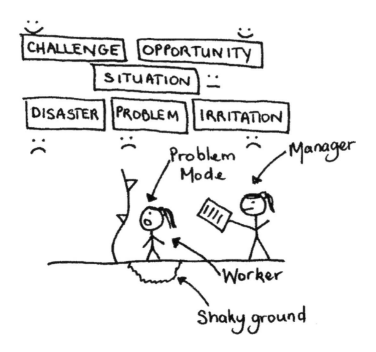

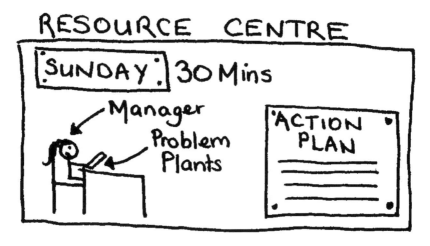

STEP 9: WIDER GARDEN VISION

Developed a wider vision for opportunities and created the COMPOST BIN for learning from and using problems to the advantage of the whole garden.

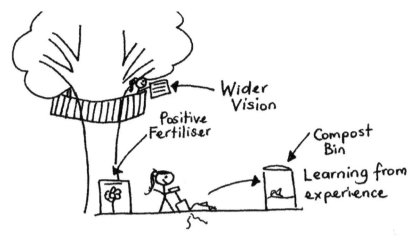

STEP 10: EXECUTIVE PROBLEM MANAGER

Became an Executive Problem Manager with exceptional 'Assessing' skills, finding positive solutions, developing acceptance and a trusted guide for others with problem plants.

You might be reading this and thinking:

"I haven't got time to do 10 steps. I haven't got time to assess all the problems I have".

Believe me, I can relate to that. That would have been my statement too, years ago. But my comeback now would be:

Just start with 30 minutes.

10 Years...

Negative Growth   or ...   Positive Growth

My problems had grown out of all proportion because I had no strategy for managing them. My mind would get tangled up and the last thing I wanted to do was spend any time with it. However, since I have taken this approach using my Thinklesticks Tool I have never looked back. I sit with my Problem Plants at least once a week. It takes me never longer than 30 minutes to assess the current issues and work out a strategy for managing them. 30 minutes rather than 112 hours a week with those nagging little problems left to fester and grow in my head.

Problems will always be arriving, sometimes from all angles. This used to frighten me into a frenzy of worry before the problems even arrived. The anticipation of the next problem was a constant low level anxiety. Yet now, after the work, the study and the experiments I have a deep understanding of dealing with situations, not enduring them.

ENDURE: Suffer something painful or difficult patiently or remain in existence, long term, unchanging. Synonyms: tolerate, suffer, submit to, learn to live with, become resigned to.

Concern can turn to worry. Worry can turn to fear. Fear can ruin gardens. Confidence can dominate worry. I now have my Garden MANAGER trained for up to Level 10 problems. That doesn't mean that I am immune to the negative emotions that those kinds of problems bring, but it does mean that I save my energy for dealing with real, serious issues instead of tangling myself up on a daily basis with every little problem imaginable (and usually they were imagined and never actually happened!). I love and respect my Situation Manager. I hope you grow to love yours too.

DESIGNER: A person who plans the look of something prior to it being made by preparing drawings or plans.
Synonyms: inventor, architect, planner, creator

My Garden DESIGNER has an interesting story of her own. She was very active in my childhood. Ambitious and creative, always making up games relating to my dream of becoming a teacher, a songwriting pop star, a dancer and a writer The dreams continued into my teenage years and I would spend hours writing and recording songs, practising dancing and I always kept that vision of being a teacher. My imagination was highly developed as a young person and I enjoyed my mind.

And then came along the damaging relationship which:

Ridiculed my songs

Discouraged my dancing

Moved me away from my friends and family

Stopped me writing through fear of judgement

A vivid, happy imagination…crushed, systematically through subtle, damaging, emotional abuse.

I had low self-esteem coming out of Secondary School. I will explain in detail in the SOIL chapter. This had a huge knock on effect to the choices I made as a 17 year old. I did not value myself or my dreams highly enough. I didn't have a loud enough voice in the relationship I found myself in. In time, the consistent negative voice in my ear, of my then husband, became the only voice that seemed to be there. My DESIGNER had run for the hills.

So between the ages of 17-21yrs was a period of survival. I was a young Mum devoted to her children but suffering the brunt of an alcoholic partner. SURVIVAL Mode really was about getting through the day. I held down an office job, and started to do well at it. Home life was volatile, stressful and difficult. I would get all of my joy from my young sons. They were everything to me. But my own well-being was suffering intensely.

You would have thought that my DESIGNER would have crept out of the woodwork at that point and thought up a vision of a better life. But no. She really had been burned.

There were no dreams. There was only survival and who was doing all the work? Little Worker Joanna.

Sadly, it took a very serious event to make Little Worker Joanna plan her escape to safety. That event, plus the previous four years had taken a massive toll on the garden as you will see in the chapter on BEANSTALKS.

So then, between the ages of 21-30 something interesting happened. I moved to Reading and wanted to make a fresh start with my boys away from the dangerous life I had been leading. I put the past behind me and vowed to be strong for my children and build a new life for us. However, my DESIGNER was still nowhere to be seen. I didn't want to dream. Dreams crashed and burned. What was the point of dreaming? It just ended in disappointment. I just had to get on with life. So what did I do?

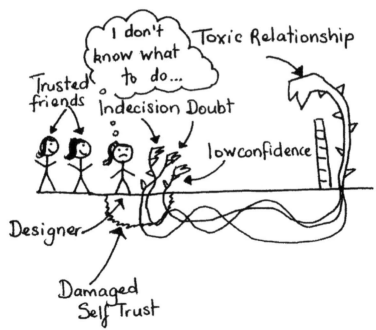

I got the DESIGNERS in. Not my DESIGNER. My dreams were not valid anymore. I didn't trust myself. I got other people to suggest designs for my garden. It was safer to ask other people's opinions. People I trusted. People who were far better at life than me. Little Worker Joanna took action, heavily guided by other people. It was much safer that way.

So I ended up:

Opening a dance school
Getting a part time classroom assistant job

Both jobs I ended up loving. They suited my skills and gifts. Thankfully the advice I took really was from people who cared about me and wanted me to be happy but my DESIGNER had absolutely no input in it whatsoever.

In fact, through my twenties I became quite resentful of my Garden DESIGNER. I'd had so many dreams as a young girl and they'd all been crushed. I didn't want to dream. Yet, strangely, she seemed very active in my boys' gardens. Inspiring them and encouraging them to do things they enjoyed. Boosting their confidence that they could do anything they wanted to do. It just hadn't worked out for me.

RESENTMENT: Bitter indignation at having been treated unfairly.
Synonyms: bitterness, irritation, dissatisfaction, discontent, grudge.

Only much later in my development process did I see it from my DESIGNER's side. Why had Little Worker Joanna stuffed up all her hard work? There was resentment from both sides. Messy.

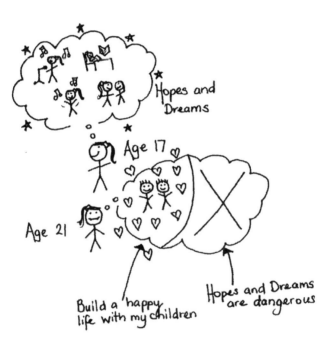

My DESIGNER finally showed up in 2005 (Age 28) when I found a book on my Mum's shelf. I'm not sure she'd ever read it all but the title intrigued me. 'Life 101: Everything We Wish We Had Learned In School - But Didn't'. I skipped to the chapter entitled "What Do You Want?" I read it with intrigue, bearing in mind I hadn't yet had my counselling or started any kind of Personal Development, but I did the exercise of writing down things that I wanted from life and then narrowed them down to a list of 10 Wants. It was actually quite a difficult process because it was then I realised how hard it was for me to dream. I didn't understand it then. I wasn't self aware. I didn't realise that my confidence had been so knocked by the past. I was just constantly annoyed and irritated at myself for being so uninspiring and lazy.

I did the exercise and for a very short period I felt a jolt of excitement that life might get better if I could achieve the things on the list. One of them was to write a book. But Little Worker Joanna was soon back to feeling demoralised because there was no time to focus on dreams (as mentioned previously) and my MANAGER was still nowhere to be seen. It once again felt more damaging to have had the dreams in the first place because it had given some level of hope, which was then dashed again. The exercise reinforced my belief that there was no benefit to having dreams. You should just get on with life and try your best to survive it.

"You get your hopes up and they just get dashed." - Little Worker Joanna (2005)

My Garden DESIGNER got her first real job in 2008. It was after the counselling and I had read 'How to be Brilliant' by Michael Heppell. I'd found the book fascinating and it had come at a time when I was feeling better able to cope with daily life after 10 months of counselling. I was open to the idea of learning more about myself and having a go at some of the exercises in the book which were practical and resonated with me. There were some activities which included using your imagination to think about how you would like life to be. Mmm. Imagination. I used to have one of those back in the day. Slowly but surely, my DESIGNER became an intermittent member of my Mind Team, along with the MANAGER who had also started to show up for work. I would say they were both Part-Time employees but any time they did show up I could feel an improvement in Little Worker Joanna's moods and motivation. However, it was a slow process. I would be determined one minute and then unmotivated the next. There was little consistency in the goal getting. Eventually this again led to despondency, my timetable got busier and I got less able to make the changes I'd wanted to. I did continue to read self development books every so often, and every time I did I would feel a benefit, but the gaps in between the work would mean I so easily slip back into the habits which were not conducive to success or happiness.

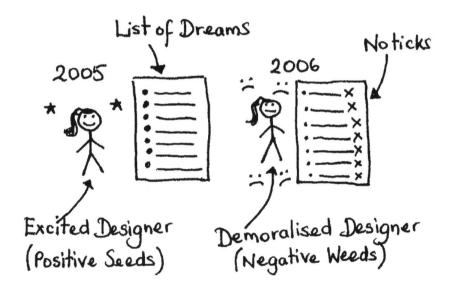

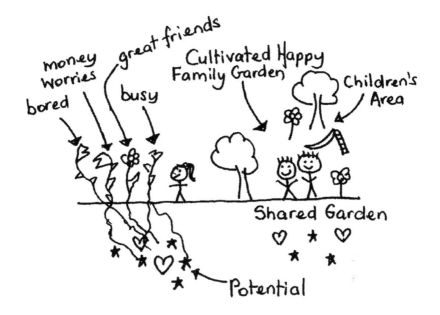

Then came 2011. The dance school was ticking along but it was difficult to get new pupils through the door due to the many dance schools in the area. I was teaching dance to the whole Primary School as well which was very rewarding and enjoyable but also quite exhausting. I was thriving in my role as a Learning Support Assistant at the Primary School, and I was looking after my boys at all other times. I had a great network of friends and on the outside... all my borders looked pretty good.

BUT...

I felt unsettled. I felt unchallenged. I felt that I was not exploring my potential, which I was starting to believe I had. The words in all the Personal Development books I was reading were starting to sink in. I found myself cutting fruit up for the children at the school for their snack times and thinking:

"I cut these bananas up every single day. I don't even like bananas." - Little Worker Joanna 2011

I would find myself day dreaming of how I could make more money with my dance teaching if I put more time and focus into it. I did love the school job but it was exhausting and draining on time and energy. I was contributing to the children and staff. I was good at it. But was it using all my skills and gifts? Was I able to stretch my own mind? No, not really. Did my current situation have a ceiling for earning potential? Yes. It was a low ceiling. For the hours and the effort I was putting in, the pay at the end of each month didn't give me and my family any freedom.

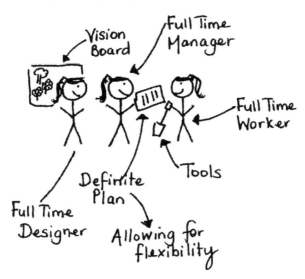

It was that feeling of unrest and my increasing interest in Personal Development that led me to an important, life-changing decision. Up until then the exercises I had done in the books were infrequent. I'd read a book and then wait a few months and read another one. The motivation wavered. It wasn't consistent. My belief in myself fluctuated. Sometimes I'd think I could take on the world. Other days I'd berate myself for being so silly. Yet, when I was in development mode, I felt so much better about life and myself. I remember writing in my journal one night in early 2011 and asking the questions:

"What if I made development a daily exercise every single day for a year? What if I study myself and do experiments all through the year? What if I commit to writing a journal every night to record the findings? What if I really take myself on as a project? What could I achieve? What if I could inspire my boys?"

Let's Do This

It was the day that my Team United. It was the day my MANAGER and DESIGNER got a Full Time Job to help assist WORKER Joanna, who didn't feel quite so little any more. With the support of the Team, she felt like things were looking up.

I started to schedule meetings with my TEAM. The WORKER, MANAGER and DESIGNER. Now this is where my previous mindset would have looked at me and said:

"How can you have a meeting with yourself?" Little Worker Joanna 2007

But this was 2011. I had decided to make myself and my life an experiment for a year. I was prepared to think outside the box. I was applying the wisdom I was reading and absorbing. I was prepared to give it a try. So I actually got a diary and scheduled meetings with my TEAM.

One of the first meetings I had was a few months after my MANAGER's discovery of TIME MANAGEMENT and the realisation of how much time I was wasting on my TV habit.

WASTING: Using or expending carelessly, extravagantly or to no purpose.
Synonyms: squander, fritter away, throw away, dissipate

I have had countless meetings since that first one. Depending on what's going on around me, I have been known to have three a day (but that's in extreme circumstances). Usually one a week is a good guide for me, on a Sunday morning. It can take 30 mins or longer depending on how I'm feeling. I value those meetings so much. It is probably the single most effective habit I can advise to practise as a NOVICE GARDENER. I could probably write an entire book about just these meetings and the value they have brought to my life but for now I will just say that this first meeting transformed my thinking and enabled me to create a life that I absolutely love. This does not mean my life is problem free, far from it. But it does mean that I have a timetable that excites me every single day and my internal world is an effective, supportive and encouraging place to be.

So, I opened a page of my journal. I could have decided to get a brand new notebook but I'm very glad that my meetings were all captured in my journals because it meant that I was able to read them back easily. I will talk about the value of CAPTURING and REVIEWING in the SOIL section.

GROWTH LABORATORY EXPERIMENT
GARDEN TEAM MEETINGS

STEP 1: PREPARE QUESTIONS
Imagine you are about to have a real meeting with people about Time Management or other subject. Think of some questions to get to the bottom of the problem.
(MANAGER)

STEP 2: DECIDE WHO IS ATTENDING
Which ROLES need to attend,

STEP 3: SCHEDULE MEETING

Make time in your schedule as you would a business meeting.

STEP 4: ANSWER THE QUESTIONS

Truthfully, honestly and from the perspective of either the DEISGNER, WORKER or MANAGER

MANAGER Sample Question: How much time have you wasted on TV this week?
WORKER Sample Answer: 23 Hours
MANAGER Sample Reply: Right, I think we need a new life strategy!

MANAGER Sample Question: What is your favourite dream at the moment?
DESIGNER Sample Answer: To live in a bigger house
MANAGER Sample Reply: Right, I'll have a brainstorm of ideas on how this can be achieved.

STEP 5: ASSESS and ADDRESS

Study the answers and spend time Quality Thinking about the answers. Put together a next steps plan. Arrange another meeting if necessary.

"I have a lot to THINK about."

"How can I make this happen?"

One of the most valuable outcomes of the meetings was capturing the conflict within my own head. This had been happening all the time on my default setting without me even realising it. The meeting was just a way for those voices to come to the surface and for SELF AWARENESS to develop. We all have voices in our heads all the time. We have a commentary flowing. But I'd never stopped to analyse it properly before in a controlled environment. I liken it to a real business organisation. The workers chat and sometimes moan about the conditions. The Managers talk amongst themselves and wonder why the workers aren't doing what they should be. A void sometimes occurs between the Workers and the Managers. Usually this is because there is a communication breakdown or simply a lack of compassion and understanding on either side. Whereas the best organisations have clear lines of communication between staff and managers and value the voice of everyone. Good Managers see the gaps in skills of their workers and organise training courses. Bad Managers just get cross that the workers aren't achieving. Good Managers encourage aspirations and creativity in their workers. Bad Managers make all the rules and order people to stick to them. Even if they make little sense.

The TEAM meetings that I started to have opened the lines of communication between the roles I was playing in my mind. If the voices were going to be chatting anyway I decided that perhaps a controlled environment might be the most effective way to get better results.

Like anything in life, you get better with practise. I now know exactly how to run the meetings to get the most out of them. My Mind Garden TEAM is bigger now. But I suggest when you are starting out on your own Mind Garden journey that you begin with the core three. The MANAGER, the DESIGNER and the WORKER. You will no doubt feel as ridiculous as I did at the start. But I really do advise that you persist with this idea. I now have the belief that I was crazy NOT to do it for the first 34 years of my life!

When I looked at the WORKER role in more detail I realised that it was no wonder that I'd become overwhelmed in 2007 with no MANAGER strategically planning anything. The WORKER is the YOU that is in the everyday internal experience of life. The one that feels everything.

TYPES OF WORK

- Everyday Maintenance (Going to work, cooking, washing, tidying etc.)
- Dealing with WEEDS, BEANSTALKS and PROBLEM PLANTS (battling fears, anxieties, emotions)

- Looking after SHARED AREAS in the garden (friends, relationships, family)
- Keeping everything watered (Life Balance)
- Maintenance of Borders (Keeping everything together for the outside world.)
- Development Workers (Working on new projects for the garden)
- Leisure Time (Time off Work)

In 2007 most of the work in the garden was MAINTENANCE work.

MAINTENANCE: The process of preserving a condition or situation.
Synonyms: preservation, conservation, continuation, continuity, keeping up

I spent much of my days in MAINTENANCE work or trying to cut back the overgrowth. This would exhaust me so much that I'd need to relax into Leisure Time. There was very little Development Work to improve the garden and this was a big error on my part because not only did my garden become unmanageable but my worker became so unmotivated and uninspired which caused her to become disinterested and lazy.

When I think back to those days, I am not sure how I managed to cope. There was no organisation, all thoughts were jumbled and entangled together. I lived very much in REACTIVE mode rather than PROACTIVE.

REACTIVE: Acting in response to a situation rather than creating or controlling it.
Synonyms: supersensitive, responsive, unstable

PROACTIVE: Creating or controlling a situation rather than just responding after it has happened. Synonyms: take charge, enthusiastic

There are events in life that we cannot control and sometimes we are forced to be REACTIVE in our response but the more PROACTIVE you are, the fewer problems there seem to be to have to react to.

There is no one more PROACTIVE than the GREENHOUSE SPECIALIST. I employed her in 2011. What a life changing and exciting member of the TEAM.

I will go into more detail about the role that my GREENHOUSE plays in my life in a later chapter, but just to give you a brief insight, it is where random ideas/dreams/thoughts are developed in a controlled and protected environment to see if and how an idea could grow from that little seed of a thought.

In the past, I would often have a flash of inspiration but because my SOIL (Self Esteem) was so unhealthy, I knew it wouldn't grow into anything so I'd dismiss it and forget about it. Every so often I might think about it again and possibly again but I never actually did anything about it. It would end up in the WHAT A WASTEBIN.

When I studied GOAL ACHIEVEMENT, I learnt that there is an important process when you get ideas flash into your head. I have developed the GREENHOUSE Analogy to support this process and it really is one of my favourite places to be in my MIND GARDEN.

The GREENHOUSE SPECIALIST learned on the job. She started with a small seed, took the advice from various sources of wisdom on how to achieve success and was astounded by the joy of watching the seedling grow big enough to then transfer into the MAIN GARDEN to flourish. She has now gained and continues to gain skills in the area of growing ideas from tiny seeds. Sometimes the seeds come straight from my DESIGNER and sometimes they come from unknown sources! An idea will just flash across my mind. I'm fascinated by this. I know there is discussion to be had about whether these are religious or spiritual voices guiding me, the stars and universe aligning, or whether it is just my best and highest self being very clever! I have heard it described as the 6th Sense, The Subconscious Mind, God (with various names and religions), Imagination, Hunches and many other things. I understand that everyone has their own opinion on this, their own beliefs and some people are like me and are undecided. The great thing I've realised is that for me, it doesn't matter where it springs from. If it's a good idea, and it's worth growing, I will put it in my GREENHOUSE and my GREENHOUSE SPECIALIST will look after and nurture it.

I think we all have little thought seeds every single day. Some are positive and some are negative. When I wasn't managing my mind it was pot luck what actually grew from the variety of thoughts in a day, week, month, year, and decade. I have to say, I think the negative seeds had more natural strength, supported by the dry and damaged soil, giving those negative seeds an environment to grow strong and fast in the form of WEEDS and BEANSTALKS. Positive seeds need far more care and that is the key role of the GREENHOUSE SPECIALIST. Her role is to NURTURE.

NURTURE: Care for and protect (someone or something) while they are growing. Help and encourage the development of.
Synonyms: attend to, look after, support, feed, nourish, cultivate, advance, boost, assist, help, strengthen, encourage

The opposite of NURTURE is NEGLECT.

NEGLECT: Fail to care for properly. Not pay proper attention to, disregard, fail to do something.
Synonyms: uncared for, abandoned, untended, lose sight of, discount, overlook, forgotten, unnoticed, unappreciated, disrepair

The Latin meaning of the word makes even more sense in Garden Terms.

Neg- not
Legere - choose, pick up

I'm now so passionate about those little positive seeds whereas in the past I neglected to pick them up and nurture them into something special. I'm so glad that I realised the importance of developing the GREENHOUSE SPECIALIST role within my TEAM. My GARDEN is unrecognisable due to her hard work.

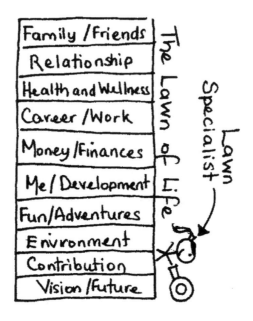

I adapted this idea for the MIND GARDEN because I find it beneficial to check in on my LAWN OF LIFE every few months to see how things are looking. The LAWN SPECIALIST is an ANALYST. She ASSESSES the lawn closely and sees where things might need attention. In my experience there are usually one or two areas which may be starting to dry up and so by doing regular lawn checks, I can make changes and implement new strategies before the whole area dries up completely. If one area of the LAWN is dying, it can affect the whole feel of your life and mind. I've learned the importance of assessing and addressing things regularly to avoid unnecessary stress later on. I would say that the LAWN SPECIALIST is employed to do 4 checks a year. It's one of those jobs which if you were to analyse it every single day it could feel overwhelming but it is very useful to just keep a check as every new season approaches.

As with any team in an organisation TEAM MORALE is vitally important to success and happiness. My one Little Worker Joanna was suffering from very low morale at the worst point when she had no back up, no guidance, no positive internal communication and very little hope of change.

MORALE: The confidence, enthusiasm, and discipline of a person or group at a particular time. Synonyms: confidence, self-esteem, team spirit, state of mind, optimism, hope, determination.

The attitude of the TEAM is also vitally important to the effectiveness of the work that gets done in the garden. Attitude is often linked to the way we interact with other people. If someone has a bad attitude then we know about it. You pick up on the negative vibe straight away. However, I know that I had not picked up on my Inner Attitude for a very long time. Now I listen to it. If my WORKER is showing a LAZY or UNINSPIRED attitude, there is probably a reason behind it so my MANAGER will question:
"Why are you feeling like this today?"
To which the reply could be any number of things...
"I'm feeling overwhelmed."
"I didn't sleep well."
"The sun isn't shining."
"My period just started."
"I don't know really."

It is then very important that the MANAGER responds with a GOOD and ENCOURAGING ATTITUDE:

"Ok, let's work out why it's overwhelming and help with that first."

"Ok, let's plan a power nap during the day."

"Let's make the sun shine internally instead then with some happy music."

"Periods are very annoying. Let's not expect too much from today. Any progress will be a bonus."

"Ok, let's get 5 things done and then reassess how it's feeling."

If the MANAGER has a bad attitude it can be damaging to the TEAM MORALE:

"Oh stop being so stupid."

"You should have gone to bed earlier. You always do this."

"You are always complaining."

"Stop being so pathetic."

"Buck you ideas up. You are so annoying."

ATTITUDE: Your attitude to something is the way that you think and feel about it, especially when this shows in the way you behave.
Synonyms: point of view, frame of mind, outlook, perspective, stance, position, ideas, beliefs, interpretation

A very powerful thing I have learned through Personal Development is that the way I wake up can directly affect the entire day if it is not controlled, managed or adjusted intentionally by a good morning routine. I do believe it is pot luck how I feel when I wake. If I see the sun poking through the blinds, I instantly feel more positive. If I didn't sleep well, I instantly have a feeling of dread that it's going to be a long day. These are all natural states and human nature. But those things can directly affect my attitude for the day if I don't disrupt them. It's all fine if I wake up in a positive, bright and determined mood but if I wake in a negative mood I now know the damage that can do to my garden and neighbouring gardens if left unchecked.

A bad attitude can have such wide reaching effects on the garden. A bad mood or emotion is different from a bad attitude. Things cannot possibly be good all the time. There are going to be tough times but even through the bad times, you can choose to have a good attitude. I have heard many times...

Attitude is everything.

I do believe attitude affects everything. Your inner attitude can have a massive impact on the internal enjoyment of a moment, a relationship, an encounter, an hour, a day, a month and ultimately, a lifetime. An outer attitude can have long and lasting effects on other people's gardens too. I will cover this more in the GARDEN BORDERS and SHARED AREAS sections.

When I studied the effects of ATTITUDE, I never saw things in the same way again. I had not monitored my attitude before 2007. I never linked my attitude in any given circumstance to the outcome. I would just very quickly lay the blame on the event or the people involved if it did not go my way.

People now often say to me:

"You are such a positive person."

I like to think this is because I work daily on my POSITIVE ATTITUDE. This does not mean that things are always positive in my life. It does not mean I say something is positive when it's not. What I do try to do is bring my positive attitude to as many situations as possible because I know the benefit that this brings to myself and to others.

GROWTH LABORATORY EXPERIMENT
Check Morale and Attitude Daily

STEP 1: CHECK MOOD AND ATTITUDE IN THE MORNING

STEP 2: ASK... HOW AM I FEELING TODAY?

STEP 3: ASK... IS THIS GOING TO BE HELPFUL OR HARMFUL TO MY GARDEN AND OTHERS TODAY?

STEP 4: IF IT'S HARMFUL WHAT CAN I DO ABOUT IT?

I have studied a lot of Tony Robbins' Personal Development work. I could listen to the man for hours and often do as his outlook on our own personal responsibility for our lives is inspiring. I believe now that it is my personal responsibility to set up my ATTITUDE every morning of every day. It takes 5 minutes. Sometimes I do it as part of my Journal Work in the morning but other times I can be sitting having breakfast and just do a quick internal check in my mind.

ATTRIBUTES: A quality or feature regarded as a characteristic or inherent part of someone or something. Synonyms: quality, feature, characteristic, trait, hallmark, distinction

Latin Roots: Adtribuere

Ad - to
Tribuere - assign

In 2011, I clearly remember reading a paragraph about Positive Attributes. It was suggesting you write down a list of positive things about yourself to balance up with the negative. I believe it was an exercise for improving Self Confidence and Self Image. Well... I sat there... with a blank look on my face. Positive Attributes? I probably should have known what that meant but as with many things, I had to look it up. OK. So, I discovered there are positive and negative attributes to the human character. That made sense.

I researched online and found a list of Primary Personality Traits which could also be described as Attributes if they were assigned to your personality. I had come to my own conclusion that the only positive traits I could think of were that I was:

Nice
Kind
Caring

I was a nice person. I was kind to people. I cared deeply for my boys, family and friends. So my GARDEN TEAM were nice, kind and caring to other people. Well, that was a good start. I wasn't a horrible person.

What I had printed out was a long list. 638 Personality Traits! Really? This was interesting.

Positive Traits 237

Neutral Traits 292

Negative Traits 292

Firstly, I didn't agree with them all. Some of the negative traits I would have thought were positive. Some of the positive traits I would have called negative. Some of the neutral traits I would have put in either positive or negative. It was a fascinating task to look through them and think about what each word meant to me.

I was being completely honest with myself. I resonated with more negative personality traits than positive in 2011. I wasn't showing the list to anyone. It was only me who knew. It was a truthful, real and profound moment when I wrote down the words that I felt I could "assign" to me, that I could "attribute" to me, that were my "attributes" on that particular day in my history. I am sure that had other people been around me at the time they would have tried to convince me that I wasn't some of those negative things and that I had more positive traits BUT this was about how I FELT about myself as a WORKER, MANAGER and DESIGNER. This was about my TEAM's QUALITIES and FLAWS through my eyes.

Anxious, bewildered, bland, cautious, confused, cynical, delicate, dependent, discontented, disorganised, easily discouraged, foolish, hesitant, indecisive, insecure, irritable, lazy, paranoid (mild), procrastinating, reactionary, regretful, resentful, tense, undisciplined, unimaginative, vulnerable, weak, empathetic, good-natured, kind, sensitive.

Thank goodness for the last few. It's better to end on a high!

These were the words that I assigned to myself (the WORKER) that day. It really was a truthful day. Thankfully, I had also been studying the amazing work of Ralph Waldo Trine "Character Building Thought Power", written in 1899. If I hadn't listened to that around the same time as doing this exercise I might have felt more depressed than when I'd started! But Ralph's words were heartwarming to me. Character building suggested that attributes can be developed. I am living proof that they can. I am also here to tell you that the process can be a lot of fun! I extracted what was helpful to me from Ralph. Not all of it applied to me but much of it did. The most striking of all was that the characteristics I was displaying were having a direct effect on my MIND GARDEN and in turn, my life.

GROWTH LABORATORY EXPERIMENT
Character Building (Team Training)

STEP 1: CHOOSE A POSITIVE TRAIT TO EMULATE
I chose DISCIPLINE

STEP 2: CHOOSE A GOAL TO PRACTISE THE TRAIT
I chose to write every day for 30 minutes.

STEP 3: CHOOSE THE VOICE OF YOUR CHOSEN TRAIT
I battled with the lazy voice and practised listening to the DISCIPLINED voice over and over and over and over, even when it was the hardest thing to do.

STEP 4: PERSIST WITH THE TRAINING
Now start to apply trait to other areas of life and not just the goal.

I did. It was surprising that once I had done the initial training in DISCIPLINE I was able to apply it more easily to every area.

STEP 5: CONTINUE OVER TIME TO PRACTISE
Eventually... I became DISCIPLINED

Yay! I had won a positive attribute. The positive effects on my MIND GARDEN were astounding.

I have to say that some ATTRIBUTES are harder than others. It is also essential that I take inventory of my attributes at least once a year because nasty little habits can creep in if you are not intentionally managing your mind regularly. I will forever thank Ralph for one of my favourite quotes:

"I will be what I **will** to be."

The more POSITIVE ATTRIBUTES I trained in, the higher the TEAM MORALE seemed to be and the easier life became.

As you understand the MIND GARDEN in more depth you will come to realise that every positive improvement in one area often has a knock on effect to other areas. As I increased my POSITIVE ATTRIBUTES through consistent and intentional training I could see with clarity that it was having an enormously beneficial impact on everything, especially the very important... SOIL.

2. SOIL

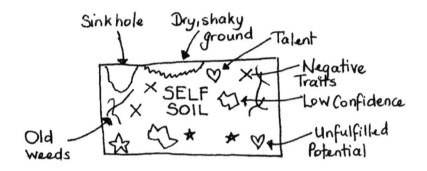

Well, what can I say about SOIL? In The Mind Garden Analogy SOIL is by far the most complex area and also, in my opinion, the most important. Before I decided to take myself on as a project, I used to say to people:

"I've lost my confidence." Little Worker Joanna 2007

But when I delved into the area of Confidence I realised what a wide subject it is. I decided that the SOIL in the garden would be all the Self Attributes, Personality Traits, Abilities, Flaws and Gifts that make up who we are, which in turn affects what we can or cannot grow in our Gardens.

NOURISH: Provide with the food or other substances necessary for growth, health and good condition.
Synonyms: feed, provide for, sustain, enhance the fertility of, care for, supply, support

STARVE: If you are starved of something necessary or good, you do not receive enough of it.
Synonyms: deny oneself, cease, constrain, be deficient

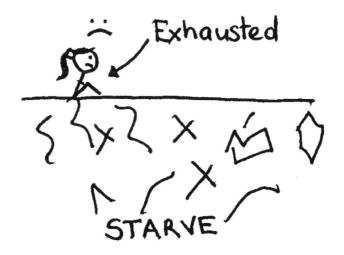

In real life gardens, the soil makes an incredible difference to whether something grows easily and flourishes or whether weeds are likely to manifest and take over. So many natural factors are at play including location, climate and minerals and left to its own devices, soil can either be effective or not. A keen gardener will know their soil and if there is a part of the garden that is dry, they will water it, if it needs a bit of attention, they will give it a good dig, if they need to replace it altogether, they'll go and buy a brand new bag of compost. Knowledge and awareness are the keys to good soil management. I have come to realise that this is the same for the SOIL in the MIND GARDEN.

If you nourish yourself and your needs, the garden is more likely to flourish. If you neglect and starve your needs, you are more likely to suffer. Yet I did not intentionally make myself suffer. I hadn't realised the importance of looking after my soil. I had no idea that I could be in control of so many things within it. I just thought confidence was something you won and lost. I used to have it. Then I didn't. Life had been difficult. It took me a long time and a lot of studying to understand how important taking responsibility for your own SOIL really is.

As with most of the ideas in the MIND GARDEN analogy, I have become fascinated with how personalities are made up and why people choose certain attitudes and behaviours which either NOURISH or STARVE their soil.

It is hard to write this chapter because the subject matter is so large. I am constantly tweaking and enhancing my knowledge, insight and understanding but all I can do is pass   on   what   I   have   learned   so   far.

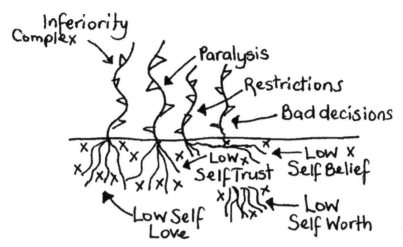

At my most depressed and entangled, my self-esteem and confidence were very low. The paralysis and restrictions of not believing in myself, not liking or trusting myself, not being able to look myself in the mirror without feelings of disgust rise up and not feeling worthy of any effort to change. Feeling too weak to do anything about it just makes you even more frustrated. All the time putting on a front to the world that you are absolutely fine which, in turn, makes you feel like a complete fraud. An awful cycle of self-destruction. If you are reading this and it resonates with how you feel now, I want you to know there is hope and so much more to live for but I truly understand the darkness. Knowing there are other people in the world suffering as I did, internally, has made me even more determined to make Thinklesticks a household name. I want the doodles to reach out to people and let them know they are understood on a deep level. I know how important it was for me to find words that understood me but they were few and far between. I want to be another voice in the world to prove that no matter how low you feel now...there is a way to feel better. It will be your own unique path...but you can do it.

What is SOIL in the MIND GARDEN analogy?

Well, simply put it is:

- How you feel about yourself and your belief systems.
- Your natural gifts, talents, interests, flaws, skills

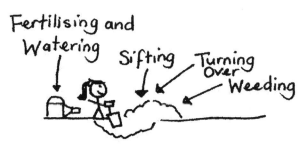

Those can be broken down into so many different things, just like real soil in the ground. If you dig in a real garden, just one little trowel of earth, you will find a hundred different minerals, bugs, little stones, compost, dry bits, moist bits, fertile sections, dying sections, unwelcome litter that someone threw in there years ago, and sometimes you will come across true gems and diamonds but you normally have to dig deep for those. A real life gardener would dig at the soil before planting something. They would analyse whether the soil needed attention, sifting, turning over, weeding, fertilising and watering before they could plant the new item with confidence that they'd done all they could do to encourage good growth.

FOUNDATIONS: An underlying basis or principle for something.
Synonyms: basis, starting point, fundamental, core, heart, essence, underpinning, groundwork

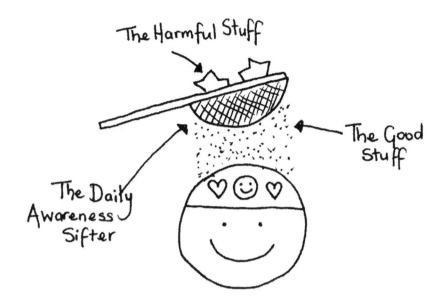

The SOIL is really like the heart and soul of the MIND GARDEN. It is complex, vast and can be affected by so many different things. I hope that in this chapter I am at least able to highlight the importance of regular SOIL checks and encourage DAILY SIFTING. It's a dream of mine that one day, the world will sift their minds daily, every single one of us. The benefit of SIFTING to my life has been so powerful. I will go into it in more depth later but now that I understand that my 2007 messy, uncontrollable, depressing, dark, weed-ridden, dried-up-soil filled MIND GARDEN was a direct result of NOT SIFTING through my mind at the end of the day; I will NEVER leave my SIFTER unused for more than three days. Because even three days, is too long.

I highlighted very early on in my Personal Development journey that my SELF ESTEEM and SELF CONFIDENCE were very low. I am grateful to my younger self that I decided to study this area and try to understand it. I was a little overwhelmed at first by what I uncovered.

There are so many aspects of confidence and self esteem.

I started to read about how confidence and self esteem can vary so much depending on what area of life you are looking at. For instance, I had lost confidence in my ability to dance after such a long break, but because it was an area where I was naturally gifted and talented (that may sound boastful but it is an honest reflection of knowing myself), my confidence and self esteem was soon restored in this area, once I spent a bit of time developing my skills again. However, my ability to walk into a room and feel confident talking to strangers without having a constant negative self-talk telling me how ugly I was and how everyone else was doing better at life than me, took much longer to address because the issue was much deeper and contained many weeds and toxicity in the soil surrounding those feelings of inadequacy and inferiority.

I have spent many hundreds of hours contemplating the effects of low self-esteem and confidence. I've analysed how it affected my own life, the lives of those around me, the lives of the people I have interviewed in my Research Project and then the wider implications of this as a nation, a continent, the world and ultimately as a human species. It has obviously been an ongoing struggle for humans because so much literature and wisdom has been left behind for us to pick up and study. So many wise words are out there, yet they are not as easy to find as you would think they would be. I've had to dig for the gold but then I had a personal desire to understand it. Now that I do have a much greater understanding, I am so confused as to why we are not taught it all at school, at university, at regular MIND CHECKS that should be set up like the physical health checks we are offered on the NHS. A whole overview to see how you are doing, before the breakdowns occur, before the depression has well and truly set in, before the addictions are allowed to take hold, before the anxieties and panic disorders claim their power over the gardens and their workers.

Although I am a firm believer that it is the role of every human being to take responsibility for their own gardens (to the best of their own unique ability), I also believe that we are being very badly let down by society because we are not being guided, supported, encouraged or indeed, taught how to do this effectively for ourselves.

I think there is a positive movement at the moment which is talking about Mental Health with much less stigma. There is increasing awareness of the benefits of counselling and CBT to support people when they are struggling. However, I am seeing first hand, with young people, that the increasing stress and pressure put on them at such a young age is causing breakdowns in coping mechanisms much younger and, indeed, much more severely than ever before. It is not just young people. It is people from all walks of life. Many are walking around in their daily lives appearing to be fine, yet internally are living a very different experience, as I did.

SOIL is not just on the surface. It goes deep underground. You can keep the surface looking neat and tidy quite easily. It is far harder to keep the true foundations as healthy looking without effective tools and knowledge on how to do it.

So I developed my SOIL ANALYSIS tool as an easy way for me to keep a check of my overall feelings about myself. It is one of my favourite tools. I am always upgrading it when I find out new information which may help to understand myself and others better. I do not claim to know it all. I think I will always be learning, thinking, mulling things over, experimenting and exploring in this area of the garden because there is always more insight to gain.

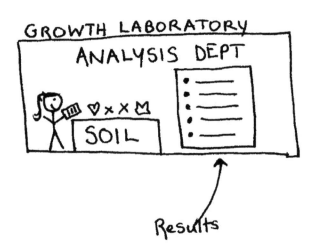

GROWTH LABORATORY EXPERIMENT
Soil Analysis

STEP 1: READ ALL DESCRIPTIONS OF THE SELF SOIL (Self Esteem/Self Confidence etc.

STEP 2: RATE HOW YOU ARE FEELING ABOUT EACH OF THEM ON A SCALE OF 0-10

This is a general feeling you get when you think about the word. Go through each ot the 16 Self Words. Honesty is the best policy because it is only for your benefit. If the numbers are low they can be increased in time. 0 is nonexistent. 10 is extremely healthy.

STEP 3: ADD UP ENTIRE SCORE

That is your SOIL ANALYSIS DATA (General) for today.

SELF SOIL
Self Acceptance 0-10

An individual's satisfaction or happiness with oneself. Self acceptance involves self-understanding, a realistic, albeit subjective, awareness of one's strengths and weakness.

Self Respect 0-10

Pride and confidence in oneself; a feeling that one is behaving with honour and dignity.

Self Esteem 0-10

Confidence in one's own worth and abilities. How you feel about yourself.

Self Belief 0-10
An individual's ability to believe in themselves.

Self Love 0-10
Regard for one's own well-being and happiness

Self Assurance 0-10
Someone who has self assurance shows confidence in the things that they say and do because they are sure of their abilities.

Self Determination 0-10
The process by which a person controls their own life.

Self Confidence 0-10
The feeling of being secure in yourself and your abilities.

Self Trust 0-10
To be able to rely on one's resources (i.e. emotional, mental and physical)

Self Knowledge (0-10)
Understanding of oneself or one's own motives or character.

Self Reliance
Reliance on one's own powers and resources rather than those of others.

Self Awareness 0-10
Conscious knowledge of one's own character and feelings.

Self Discipline 0-10
The ability to make yourself do things you know you should do even when you do not want to.

Self Care 0-10
The actions that individuals take for themselves, on behalf of and with others, in order to develop, protect, maintain and improve their health, wellbeing and wellness.

Self Worth 0-10
The sense of one's own value or worth as a person.

Self Image 0-10
The idea one has of one's abilities, appearance and personality.

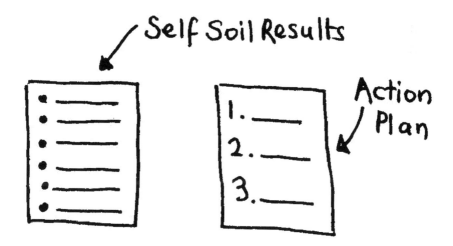

The first time I did an exercise like this it was only for Self Confidence, Self Esteem, Self Belief and Self Trust. I scored myself 4 out of a possible 40. It was grim. The last time I completed my own SELF SOIL ANALYSIS I scored 128/160. No number was lower than a 6. I know my SOIL is healthy because I work on it. I've learnt how to. It's not perfect, because I'm a human being, but it is very effective and it allows me to grow a flourishing garden and most importantly, it allows me to enjoy it. We will use the data later!

I mentioned earlier that the scale from 0-10 suggests that 10 is a very healthy number. When I was studying Self Esteem and Confidence, I read a lot about the damaging effects of low self esteem, how life could be vastly improved with healthy self esteem but also about how if your esteem over inflates this can have negative social implications. So I made a Thinklestick to remind me of this because I did not want to have a garden where my soil was so watered that it then became soggy, swampy and unattractive. There is a fine line between having healthy self esteem; knowing your worth, trusting yourself, believing in your own ability, taking care of yourself, feeling happiness and joy in your accomplishments, having the inner strength to be your true self to that of having high self esteem where you value your self far more than you value everyone else.

The word that helps to remind me that although I am important, I am no more important than anyone else is:

HUMILITY: The feeling or attitude that you have no special importance that makes you better than others. Synonyms: humbleness, modesty

I love this word. There are different interpretations of it but I think it is a great word for humanity. You may have more knowledge than someone about a particular subject, you may have a nicer car or a more expensive house, you may have more money or more sense than someone else, but that doesn't put you on a pedestal and make you more important than anyone else on the planet. You may bring more value to others but it doesn't make you or your opinion more important than anyone else.

Humility does not stop me striving to be my best, to do my best, to stretch myself or share my happiness and achievements with others but it does stop me feeling better than other people. It keeps me grounded. It keeps me...

Down to earth.

I read a lot about humility in a fantastic book called "Aspire" by Kevin Hall. That book taught me the value that words can bring to your life. As you can see in Thinklesticks, I like to unpick words, find their roots and really get to know them. I then assess what they mean to me, how I relate to them and often they teach me about myself and life.

Another wonderful word that "Aspire" brought into my life and MIND GARDEN is:

GENSHAI: You should never treat yourself or another person in a manner that makes one feel small.

It is an ancient Hindi word. It is such a powerful word to learn, understand and practise. It is very appropriate for the SOIL chapter. If you treat yourself small, it is as if you don't matter, you don't count, and you are not worth the effort. You are damaging your own self SOIL. If you treat others small, you make them feel as if they don't matter, their feelings don't count, they are not worth the time or effort. You are damaging their self SOIL. Genshai is the perfect balance. You know your worth, you know you are special and important… yet you also know that every other person you meet has worth and is special and important too. Even if their behaviours, habits, personalities or actions do not fall in line with yours, genshai brings you back down to earth.

When you practise genshai, you can very easily spot someone who has low self esteem. If that is the case, I believe it is even more important to leave that person a little better than you found them. Everyone has their own MIND GARDEN to manage. Just as we can all have a positive or negative effect on our own SOIL we also have the same amount of power to affect other people's.

Genshai

Genshai

Now onto one of my favourite topics in the MIND GARDEN - GIFT SOIL.

GIFT: A natural ability or talent.
Synonyms: talent, flair, ability, power, genius, strength, brilliance

Personal Development has done something truly beautiful for me. It took me from a dark, troubled, entangled place and guided me, with wisdom, to a place where now I spend most of my gardening time digging at my potential in my GIFT SOIL.

At my worst time, I believed all my potential had died with the person I used to be before I got married. But how wrong could I be?

The trouble with GIFT SOIL is that it is sometimes buried deep within the ground. Especially if life events happen to prevent you from developing the area. Sometimes criticism can cause you to lose your confidence and the gift soil dries up because it's fed with fear instead of faith. If WEEDS or BEANSTALKS get in the way of letting anything in your GIFT SOIL area really flourish to its full potential, it can limit your belief about how much talent you really have.

I kept hearing about the story 'Acres of Diamonds' in various development books. It was an essay and speech by Russell H Conwell which he delivered over 6,152 times in his lifetime. It was first published in 1890.

If you have never read it, I recommend it. The message resonates with me greatly. I used to think that if I became someone else, or tried to make my garden look like everybody else's it would bring me happiness and fulfilment. I have learned that all I had to do was look in my own garden and I would find my very own Acres of Diamonds. I had to clear the garden first, so that I wasn't spending all my energy chopping back harmful weeds every day but once they had been removed and the soil nourished, I was able to start using my energy to dig deep into my GIFT SOIL and discover my potential. This, I feel, is where the magic happens.

We all have innate abilities, strengths, characteristics and talents. We can put our minds to improve and develop any attributes that we choose but there is no denying that we all have different levels of natural ability in varying areas. Not just ability but interest. We all find different things inspiring or attractive. Some people are drawn to red, others are drawn to blue.

I have come to the realisation in my own MIND GARDEN that there is a perfect combination soil which helps dreams and goal plants grow joyfully and happily and with the greatest fulfilment factor.

HEALTHY SELF SOIL +
GIFT SOIL =
THE MOST BRILLIANT THINGS

And those brilliant things sprinkle more fresh nutrients into the SELF SOIL which keeps it healthy and not depleted, so the happy cycle can start again

I have become fascinated with POTENTIAL as I journey through my own Personal Development. My understanding of it is very much linked to GIFT and SELF SOIL. I think back to when my belief in myself was so low. I would never have taken on the big projects that I have in more recent years if I still had that negative and unhelpful view of myself. Yet, all the time, deep down in the earth of my garden, was all that POTENTIAL. Thankfully, I DID take myself and my garden on as a project and I have learned how to dig at my potential, develop my natural GIFTS and start to grow things in those areas. When you stop and think about it, POTENTIAL really is an exciting thing. Well it is when you are feeling confident. It can be distressing if you are not. Unfulfilled POTENTIAL can lead to regret. Unused GIFTS can lead to boredom and even depression.

All I know is that I have found so much happiness in digging at my POTENTIAL and planting things in my GIFT SOIL. I do believe also that this is where I am able to contribute most to the world around me. Things that come naturally to me are also things that I love to do.

POTENTIAL: Having or showing the capacity to develop into something in the future. Latent qualities or abilities that may be developed and lead to future success or usefulness.
Synonyms: possible, future, budding, developing, dormant, undeveloped, possibilities, capacity, power, talent, flair

Having spoken at length with many people in my Research Project, this word means even more to me now. I have listened to people who don't believe in themselves enough to dig at their POTENTIAL. The reasons vary. It could be that the SELF SOIL has been damaged over time and their confidence and self belief just isn't high enough. It could be that WEEDS of FEAR entangle them whenever they start to think they could do something, so they stop, or dumb the dream down enough for it to feel manageable. It could be that a BEANSTALK is looming over the garden, taking away the light and positivity needed to enjoy digging in the POTENTIAL plots. It could be that the TEAM is not united in some way. They are demoralised leaving the WORKER in a lazy state or simply disinterested in working due to lack of inspiration. It could be due to the lack of understanding that GIFTS and POTENTIAL require development and patience and that they don't own a GREENHOUSE to cultivate these things with care and consideration. It could be that they spend so much time concentrating on other people's gardens (family and friends) that there is not enough time allocated to their own gardens. It could be any number of things but I have discovered that it was not just me who had lost the belief in herself to achieve anything great and be useful to the world. A lot of people feel like I did. That upsets me.

My heart would ache when I heard those comments because I used to say them too. I had a garden that did not support my POTENTIAL or GIFTS. I would sit and listen and make notes of people's WEEDS and SOIL and TEAM...then I would hear snippets of inspiration and desire when they were on a subject that fired them up. I would see with clarity which development strategies and changes could be made to the garden to help.

It is why I continued to develop THINKLESTICKS. Not just for me, but for anyone who is interested in taking themselves on. I want people to look at a THINKLESTICK and be inspired because untapped potential...well...I'm not usually morbid...but it dies with you and maybe, just maybe, the world needs you at your best. The world needs your art, your songs, your kindness, your dance, your invention, your humour, your screenplay, your knitting patterns, your gadgets, your ideas, and your book. Someone, somewhere in the world, needs what you have to offer.

Another exciting area of SOIL is SKILLS. I talked about natural gifts and innate abilities but I have also discovered that I could surprise myself by studying and learning SKILLS that I had no idea I could master. These were not necessarily in my known areas of strengths. Education is a wonderful thing for the mind. Stretching yourself can be very rewarding. I used to say "I can't do that". Now I say, "I'm going to see if I can learn to do that." If I still struggle, then I will find someone who has the innate ability to do it!

So what happens next with the SOIL ANALYSIS DATA? When you have done your soul searching and established where your areas of strength and weakness lie, I would advise sitting with this information for a little while.

The best tip I can give for improving your SOIL is to become INTENTIONAL.

INTENTIONAL: Done on purpose, deliberate.
Synonyms: deliberate, conscious, intended, purposeful, aforethought

Actions and habits form over time. They can be good or bad, conscious or unconscious, helpful or harmful. Often I would not even know why I was doing certain things. They had just become habits because I was not living intentionally. I did not have a guiding system, a goal to strive for, attributes to aspire to or my MIND GARDEN to unify my thinking and understanding of happiness. Those actions and habits over time were generally not good for my SOIL or indeed any part of my internal experience of life.

Development taught me a way to train myself to be intentional. When you are reminded that every action, every word, every moment, every interaction has a consequence, it can be a powerful realisation. Are your actions and habits helpful or harmful to the enjoyment of your MIND GARDEN? Are the actions and habits of those around you helpful or harmful to the enjoyment of your MIND GARDEN?

In 2011 when I had decided to spend a bit of time every day on my own development I designed myself a "Degree of Happiness". The protagonist in my second novel 'Benchmark II' (to be published) also takes this path! At this point I knew the benefits of building myself up, setting goals and having some direction but I wanted more of a structure to my learning. I didn't go to University so in my head I thought, what better degree could you possibly do than to study yourself and how to create lasting happiness and peace of mind. I'd decided on it as a bit of fun. Little did I know that it would actually have such a profoundly positive effect.

As I am a teacher at heart, I found it fun to design my modules. It wasn't rigid. I did not have to do 2000 word essays. I would choose an area of life to focus on. Either for a day, a week, a month, 6 months or a year. Sometimes I'd have two subjects running alongside each other. Basically, it was a guiding system for my own learning. I would record information in my journals and also gather inspiration in there from sources of wisdom. It might sound very time consuming but once I got into the positive HABIT of it, I could limit it to 30 minutes a day. I often carried on for longer or had chunks in my day that I used. The most important thing was that I was intentionally focusing on an area and ASSESSING and ADDRESSING and RECORDING my findings.

The GROWTH LABORATORY became a wonderful place. It was fascinating learning about human behaviour, emotional and social intelligence, communication, setting goals, attributes, belief systems, confidence, leadership, potential and many other things. I loved my experiments and would often share them with friends. I still make sure I enter the GROWTH LABORATORY regularly. Progress brings me happiness. When I learn something in the GROWTH LABORATORY and implement positive action because of it,

I feel that I improve. I'm an upgraded version of myself. I still have the glitches in software but each time I upgrade, the glitches iron out and it makes life and the MIND GARDEN better.

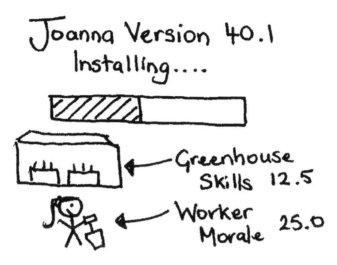

Something I used to do constantly was compare myself to others. I would enter a room and instantly judge the way I was dressed compared to how everyone else looked, or how ugly I was in comparison to the beautiful faces around me. Even if I had experienced a nice time, laughter, connection and fun with the people I'd been in the room with, it would have been a mostly damaging experience for my SELF SOIL. Why? Because I had felt INFERIOR. My mind had been focused on an inner scale of JUDGEMENT and I would almost certainly end up on the negative side of it.

One day, I decided to do an experiment to find out how my SELF TALK was not helping my SOIL.

GROWTH LABORATORY EXPERIMENT
The Comparison Trap

STEP 1: AWARENESS MONITOR

From the moment you wake up until the time you go to sleep imagine you have a monitor on you. Each time you hear your mind comparing or feeling inferior you must make an inner note to be recorded at the end of the day.

STEP 2: ANALYSE THE RESULTS

Was the SELF TALK helpful or harmful? Were there patterns? Are you a critic or a cheerleader?

STEP 3: ADDRESS THE FINDINGS

Try to replace the negative talk with a more positive approach on a regular basis. Set goals in social situations.

STEP 4: MONITOR REGULARLY

Repeat often.

STEP 5: SPRINKLE POSITIVE RESULTS INTO SOIL

Recognise the positive results and sprinkle into the areas of Self Image, Self Esteem, Self Confidence etc.

My lab results were quite alarming. I knew I had low SELF ESTEEM and I knew I often felt INFERIOR on the inside but I had no idea to what extent I had been suffering in this state. It had also been going on for over a decade.

These were the kinds of things I would hear myself say:

"She is so pretty. Why am I so ugly? I bet everyone is thinking how ugly I am,"

"Everyone else here has life sorted. Why am I such a failure? I don't fit in here."

"I can't think of anything interesting to say. I'm so boring. I want to leave."

COMPARISON: A consideration or estimation of the similarities or dissimilarities between two things or people.
Synonyms: contrast, differentiation, weighing up

I'd heard that it wasn't a good thing to compare yourself to others but I'd done absolutely nothing about that wise piece of information when I was living in my negative default setting. Yet when I was learning about SELF ESTEEM, I was made aware of just how damaging that feeling of INFERIORITY is to the SOIL.

INFERIORITY: Lower in rank, status or quality.
Synonyms: not so important, lesser, low-grade

All the internal chatter had been left to walk all over me. I hadn't discovered the importance of SIFTING at the end of a day so all those negative comparisons fed my WEEDS and continued to damage my SOIL. The energy I would spend berating myself would be quite incredible.

There would, however, be the odd times when I'd be in a scenario where my life actually seemed better than the person I was with. In the comparison trap there were also moments of victory and validation that I wasn't doing as badly as absolutely everyone on the planet and a small bit of joy would be extracted from being around someone who made me feel better about yourself because they were doing so badly.

The COMPARISON TRAP led me to lead a life of pure chance as to whether I would feel good or bad about myself depending on how I compared to everyone around me. This was not conducive in any way to my PEACE OF MIND. I had little control over my own thoughts and feelings, especially as my SELF ESTEEM continued to get lower, resulting in the negative comparisons coming thick and fast.

The more I understood about SOIL, WEEDS and the MIND GARDEN as a whole, the more I could see that I needed to change my view on COMPARISON. It is a natural human trait. To say "Don't compare yourself to others" is actually very difficult and something I have still not mastered.

The difference is, now I use those thoughts and SIFT them into helpful inspiration for my own garden. With the use of GENSHAI, I now do this automatically. At the beginning it was difficult to shift my thinking from the negative. It had been an ingrown habit. I persisted and put INTENTIONAL effort into it as part of improving my garden. The benefits to my INTERNAL experience of life were amazing and far reaching in garden terms.

Other influences on SOIL are WEEDS and BEANSTALKS which both have chapters of their own. I still often philosophise on Sunday mornings about whether the SOIL causes the WEEDS to take hold or whether the WEEDS cause the SOIL to be damaged. It's a bit like that chicken and egg problem. The best I've come up with is that they both certainly influence each other and can strip a huge amount of joy from your MIND GARDEN.

I first drew the Daily Awareness Sifter in the summer of 2014. It was one of the Originals. I had been thinking about how the process of journaling had helped me so much by capturing ideas, emotions, successes, disappointments, mind patterns and moods as well as reactions to certain events or people. The benefits of journaling are enormous and widespread. There is no set way to do it and I have seen many different variations suggested in books. For me, all I need is a notebook and a pen. I write the date and I give the entry a title that comes naturally to me.

The first and most important benefit from journaling was my increased SELF KNOWLEDGE. I created the habit of writing an entry at the end of every day. It didn't take long and I did it after my children had gone to bed and before I went to sleep. Sometimes it would be in note form if I was pushed for time but usually, I would write at least half a page of A4. Often a full page. Then every few days I would browse back over what I'd written and that was the game changer (or Garden Changer!). The pages of the journal would reveal so much to me. They were where I really got to KNOW myself. I don't just mean knowing what I liked for dinner, knowing which friends I liked to spend time with, knowing what I was interested in. I mean, deep knowledge of what my mind was focusing on and how it was processing things. It was not a diary stating all the things I'd done that day, it was a record of how I was feeling, what I was thinking and what stood out to me as the most important parts of the day.

SIFT: Put a fine or loose substance through a sieve so as to remove lumps or large particles. Examine something thoroughly so as to isolate that which is most important. Separate something, especially something to be discarded, from something else."
Synonyms: filter, purify, refine, search through, rummage through, explore, examine, inspect, investigate, delve into, review, sort out, put to one side, weed out, remove

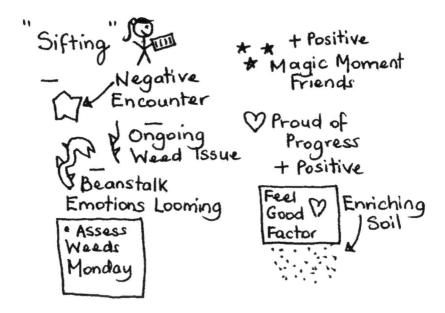

So the action of writing down the events, moods, emotions, connections and thoughts is like SIFTING the day. Reviewing what's been captured by your mind. The journaling then shakes it up and things are filtered. At first I didn't feel much benefit other than it freed my mind up a bit before bedtime. The real advantage was definitely being able to go back over the writing and pick up on things which I would have missed otherwise. For instance, I discovered that I had been a little obsessed about thinking of a love interest (unrequited) for five days running. By the sixth day I had read back over my journal and thought "This is absolutely ridiculous!" On the sixth day I distracted myself and took positive action on something I could control and had a MUCH better day. I would capture negativity. My earlier journals had a very negative slant, which ran parallel to the negative thinking. Reading back, those words had been alarming at first, but essential for my growth because it made me face up to the fact I needed to help myself.

GROWTH LABORATORY EXPERIMENT:
Daily Sifting

STEP 1: CAPTURING
Write down emotions, moods, events, communications you had through the day. Expand on the most important to you. A brief description whether it was a good or bad day overall. What is still worrying you leading into tomorrow? What were the positives?

STEP 2: ASSESSING
Return to the entry a few days or a week later and examine it closely from the MANAGER's perspective. Tick the happy, positive and constructive sentences that make

you smile. Sprinkle these into your SOIL to NOURISH it. Circle or highlight areas of concern, recurring themes, negative interactions and then spend time assessing these:

Is it HELPFUL or HARMFUL?
Is it TRUE or FALSE?
Is it RESOLVED or UNRESOLVED?
Is it a WEED?
Is it a BEANSTALK?
Is it a PROBLEM PLANT?
Is it a TOXIC person?
Is it a DAMAGING situation?
Is it a FEAR?
Is it SOMETHING ELSE?
Is it an ISOLATED INCIDENT or a RECURRING THEME?

STEP 3: ADDRESSING

Decide whether ACTION, EDUCATION or ACCEPTANCE is required for the highlighted areas. Make a time to plan for action or education.

STEP 4: ACCEPTANCE

For things that need ACCEPTANCE and cannot be changed put in the COMPOST BIN to get the most benefit from the NEGATIVE WASTE.

COMPOST: Decayed organic material used as a fertiliser for growing plants.
Synonyms: waste, fertiliser, humus, decompose

When I was delving deeper into creating the MIND GARDEN analogy for Thinklesticks, something came to me one Sunday Morning as I was eating a croissant. Personal Development has so many different areas but one of them is the ability to learn how to use bad experiences, emotions and situations and turn them into something more positive in the form of wisdom, compassion, understanding, self-learning, education and progress. In my earlier life I did not have this processing skill. A negative stayed a negative. It might fade a bit if I was lucky and not feel quite as thorny but it was always there. Sometimes it would even grow and get bigger (BEANSTALKS). Occasionally, I'd decide that I'd want something out of my garden, once and for all, so I'd chuck it out. The trouble was, I'd never actually dealt with it properly and it remained as toxic waste in my garden.

All this thinking and pondering led me to create the COMPOST BINS in the garden analogy. At my worst times, I did not even own a COMPOST BIN. Everything negative just lived and grew. When I was improving, I had a COMPOST BIN which I tried to discard things into but they'd just pile up. I'd ignore it and keep loading things on top until one day I wondered what that toxic stuff spilling out into my garden was? By then it's no use to the garden at all.

A main theme running through the garden analogy is that the more regularly things are CHECKED, ASSESSED, ADDRESSED and WORKED on, the more effective, efficient and less time consuming it actually is to look after, leaving more energy to spend simply enjoying life, truly from the inside out.

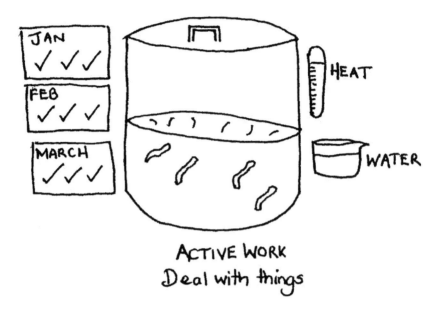

ACTIVE WORK
Deal with things

There can be many things in the COMPOST BIN at any time but it's important to look at it once a month as a guide. Check that things are improving and being broken down. If they aren't, then look at what can be done to help that process. An essential element of the COMPOST BIN is TIME. Negative things don't just disappear. For me it was comforting that I did not rush the process of breaking things down and changing things into positives because negative things have almost always been hurtful or had left high emotions. Even when you've successfully dug them out of your main garden, they linger in the COMPOST BIN for a while yet.

The main benefit of my COMPOST BIN is a real belief that things can be transformed in my mind if I work at it. Regularly. Positively. Determinedly. It may be a complex process and it takes time but it's worth the effort.

So what do you put into the COMPOST BINS? Well, that leads me nicely onto...BEANSTALKS and WEEDS...

3. BEANSTALKS

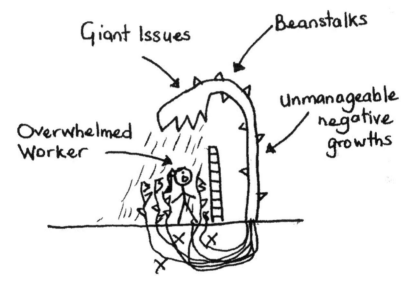

Giant Issues

Beanstalks

Unmanageable negative growths

Overwhelmed Worker

Well, this is the big one. I suppose I've been putting off writing this chapter because I know I am choosing to lay myself open to judgment with the honesty that I have decided to put into Thinklesticks. The reason I am going to let people see the depth of my internal experiences is because during the many interviews I have done so far, talking about BEANSTALKS was where people really opened up to me in a way I don't think they ever would have without this analogy. Many people have entrusted me with their deepest darkest hurt and pain that still lives and grows in some cases, because of these huge, daunting and seemingly unmanageable negative growths.

I developed this analogy with just me to base it on. I spent hundreds of hours analysing myself with a fascination and determination that I suppose was triggered by realising that knowing myself really is the very best way of helping myself. I wanted to understand why I'd made certain unwise choices along the way, or why I was suddenly suffering from anxiety from an event that happened 10 years ago. I was intrigued as to why my self esteem had dropped and how that had led to different struggles and internal suffering over a long period of time.

I have to explain that as I write about my BEANSTALKS, I do mention the impact my parents' breakup had on me. Now, this is a very difficult thing to write in a book because both my parents are very precious to me. I have strong and positive relationships with them as an adult and I also have many, many positive memories of being a child in their care but one thing I have learned on my journey so far to a flourishing MIND GARDEN is that it is very important to talk about the things that we really don't want to talk about. Something I found very empowering about using the analogy is that it actually takes things away from being so personal and lets you look objectively and analytically instead of feeling so emotionally attached. For me, it means I can be very matter of fact about things. When I talk about past events, other people are involved, but I do not lay BLAME at anyone's door. I do not hold resentment or anger because I have worked through those emotions. I've dug things up and I ACCEPT that it was just how the situation was. The thing is, when you can look at a BEANSTALK and say... "Right I can see how you've grown so big but you are not helping the enjoyment of my garden one little bit, so I'm going to chop you up, stem by stem, and put you in the COMPOST BIN", it is truly empowering.

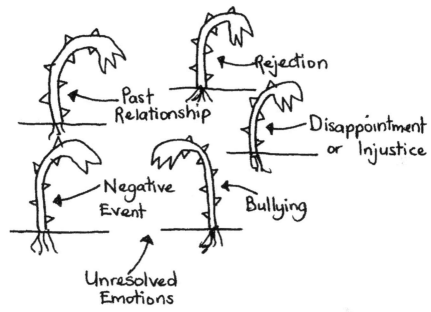

One of the horrible things about BEANSTALKS is that they have often caused a lot of hurt, anxiety, worry, fear, suffering, pain and negative consequences to the garden WORKER. If they are still alive in your garden they may also overshadow everything, or at least certain areas of the garden, and their presence is frustrating and depressing.

For me, the difficulty of BEANSTALKS was that I often did not even know they were there until they had grown so big that it was a terrifying, upsetting, confusing and traumatic event to find them. BEANSTALKS are very often the main cause of distress in a garden.

So what is a BEANSTALK? Well, it could be anything!

I have spoken to so many people about BEANSTALKS and discovered that they vary enormously from person to person. I describe them as a negative event, relationship, situation or belief that was planted (often not intentionally) in the past. At some point, you try to turn your back on it and move on. A wall is built for protection against the problem, you get on with creating a newer and better garden but behind that wall the BEANSTALK feeds on UNRESOLVED emotions, thoughts and worry. I tend to refer to BEANSTALKS as the GIANT ISSUES.

As I said, I have studied myself in so much detail that I have uncovered a wealth of knowledge about UNRESOLVED EMOTIONS and how, if left unchecked and unmanaged, they can lead to very damaging consequences for the enjoyment of the MIND GARDEN. I am choosing to share with you the BEANSTALKS that I have found in my garden so far, how they were planted, how long they grew for, how I chopped them down and how I used the compost from them to nourish my garden. I am certainly not immune from discovering BEANSTALKS in my MIND GARDEN. The last one I discovered in 2016, had been growing for 17 years. It had even got past my detection when I was highly self-aware. The wall had been cleverly hidden behind a beautiful rose bush in a section of my garden that I thought I'd dealt with. It was only when things became very confusing and upsetting in that area did I realise that a nasty thorny BEANSTALK was looming again and it had caused another bout of difficulty and struggle before I was able to remove it completely. The following pages are very visual. This is where Thinklesticks plays an important role in my life. The drawings often make far more sense to me than if I was trying to explain it in just words.

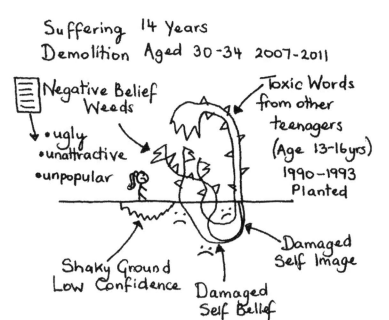

Suffering 14 Years
Demolition Aged 30-34 2007-2011

Negative Belief Weeds
• ugly
• unattractive
• unpopular

Toxic Words from other teenagers (Age 13-16yrs) 1990-1993 Planted

Shaky Ground Low Confidence

Damaged Self Belief

Damaged Self Image

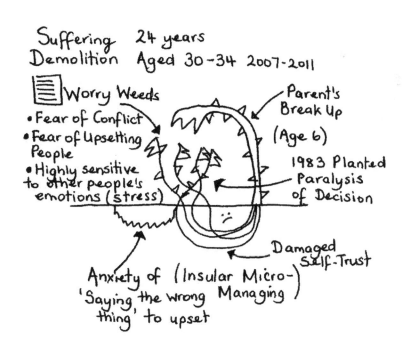

Suffering 24 years
Demolition Aged 30-34 2007-2011

Worry Weeds
• Fear of Conflict
• Fear of Upsetting People
• Highly sensitive to other people's emotions (stress)

Parent's Break Up (Age 6)
1983 Planted
Paralysis of Decision

Anxiety of 'Saying the wrong thing' to upset

(Insular Micro-) Managing

Damaged Self-Trust

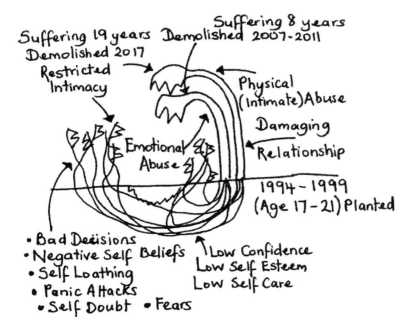

Suffering 8 years
Demolished 2007-2011

Suffering 19 years
Demolished 2017
Restricted
Intimacy

Physical
(Intimate) Abuse

Damaging
Relationship

Emotional
Abuse

1994 - 1999
(Age 17 - 21) Planted

• Bad Decisions
• Negative Self Beliefs
• Self Loathing
• Panic Attacks
• Self Doubt • Fears

Low Confidence
Low Self Esteem
Low Self Care

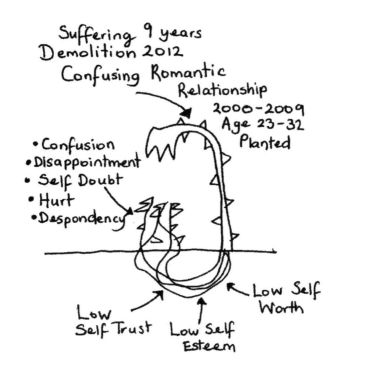

Suffering 9 years
Demolition 2012
Confusing Romantic
Relationship
2000 - 2009
Age 23 - 32
Planted

• Confusion
• Disappointment
• Self Doubt
• Hurt
• Despondency

Low Self
Worth

Low
Self Trust

Low Self
Esteem

BEANSTALK detection is often very difficult because for me a lot of the symptoms were confusing until I realised that the feelings and fears were all rooted from a past event or relationship.

I would experience what I call WEEDS on an everyday basis: annoyances, irritations, anxieties, inferiority complex, fears and often a lingering depressed feeling that I couldn't quite shift. They would leave me feeling demoralised. Weeds strip joy from my garden. Sometimes they can appear pretty and misleading but often they are just a plain nuisance. There is a whole chapter on WEEDS and how I deal with them now, but back in the difficult days I just did not know how to manage them other than constantly try, and fail, to rid the garden of them. I would make a concerted effort to change something but those WEEDS would keep popping back up time and time again.

When I developed the BEANSTALK analogy, everything began to make a lot more sense. WEEDS were often growing from the roots of the BEANSTALKS and being fed by the damaged SOIL. The best way to rid the garden of annoying WEEDS and a DARK SHADOW is BEANSTALK DEMOLITION. The longer the BEANSTALK has been growing, the more daunting it may seem to address but I believe that BEANSTALK DEMOLITION can be an incredible process of learning and enlightenment. Yes, there are often painful, difficult emotions involved but in my experience, when broken into manageable chunks it can be very rewarding and empowering to see the power of the BEANSTALK diminishing.

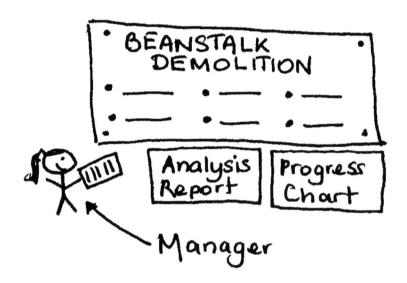

I have noticed that there is a process for successful BEANSTALK DEMOLITION in my MIND GARDEN. Now that I know this, I am not frightened of finding them. I have a firm belief in the benefit of removing them and of extracting the positives from them in my COMPOST BIN.

THE BEANSTALK PROCESS

1. A BEANSTALK seed is planted during a difficult event, relationship, encounter or period of time.

2. The emotions of that particular event, relationship or encounter are not fully healed at the time for whatever reason. Usually a case of wanting to move on or a lack of awareness of how much it hurt at the time. It could be that life is very busy and the need for distraction from the issue is stronger than the need to deal with it. It could be that you have lots of people to look after in your life and so use the energy in other people's gardens instead of your own. There are many different reasons why we do not notice that a BEANSTALK seed has been planted without our awareness.

3. Life goes on and a WALL is built.

4. WEEDS start to form in certain areas which cause sensitivity, hurt, fear, upset and pain.

5. The SOIL is weakened in those areas and sometimes it can lead to a SINKHOLE (Panic Attack, Anxiety Attack).

6. TRIGGERS for a SINKHOLE can be any number of things relating loosely or closely to the original BEANSTALK or its effects.

7. The SINKHOLE can vary in depth and darkness.

8. In other cases, no SINKHOLE appears but instead a DARK SHADOW in the form of low mood, depression and confusion which spoils the pleasure of the current garden.

9. In other cases, it can just be that WEEDS constantly entangle the WORKER making things difficult, painful and exhausting.

10. Then there will be a day when SOMETHING makes you realise things are not right. There will be a REALISATION in some form or other.

11. This is when there is a CHOICE and when

ATTITUDE can affect the outcome of discovering the BEANSTALK.

12. Choose your action plan. If it's a NEGATIVE one... repeat steps 11-12. If it's a POSITIVE one... go to step 13.

13. Implement the plan and make regular checks on the progress of the demolition.

14. Alongside the demolition, make a plan for the nourishment of SOIL.

15. Look after the WORKER during demolition times.

16. When the BEANSTALK is finally in the COMPOST BIN think about what you would like to replace it with in the main garden, as there will now be a space there.

17. Take credit for BEANSTALK DEMOLITION and know that you can cope with any BEANSTALK from here on in with this process (increased SELF-BELIEF, SELF_TRUST, SELF-KNOWLEDGE, SELF-ESTEEM, SELF-CONFIDENCE, SELF-ASSURANCE, SELF-RELIANCE etc.)

18. Make regular GARDEN CHECKS to spot BEANSTALKS and SIFT daily to ensure future BEANSTALKS are avoided where possible.

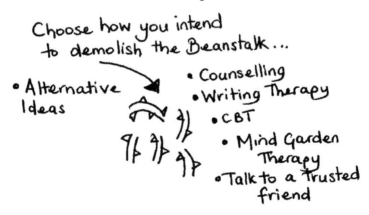

CHOICE: An act of choosing between two or more possibilities. A range of possibilities from which one or more may be chosen.

Synonyms: option, alternative, possibility, solution, selection, picking, decision, assortment

In my experience, the majority of the suffering in my MIND GARDEN comes from when I am unaware of the BEANSTALK and it is just having a negative effect on my life. The first time I discovered a BEANSTALK, it really was a terrifying time. I didn't feel that I had enough strength to cut down the daily weeds let alone have to deal with this sudden monster of a plant. It was soul destroying. Fortunately, I made a good CHOICE to take myself to counselling. I can understand why people may make other decisions at this point e.g. to isolate themselves, lean on alcohol or drugs as a way to cope. They may not seem like negative choices at all in the interim as they take away the intensity of the feelings for the WORKER much quicker than therapy or an alternative POSITIVE choice.

So number 12 in the BEANSTALK PROCESS is vital. What are you going to do now you have discovered this big, monster issue plant?

Something I believe wholeheartedly in the MIND GARDEN analogy is that no two GARDENS are the same, no two WORKERS are the same, no two TEAMS are the same and so, ultimately, no two solutions to BEANSTALKS are the same. I need to stress that the findings that I'm writing about here are drawn from my own experiences and I do not claim that my way is the high way. It works for me. It's transformed my experience of life but I believe that it is the responsibility of everyone to find their own unique skills in BEANSTALK DEMOLITION. I have faith that all BEANSTALKS can be demolished and replaced with something healthier. This does not mean you forget they were there or that they do not take time to recover from. It does not mean they are removed overnight or you forget the pain they caused. It does mean, however, that your everyday experience of the garden is far more enjoyable without them draining your resources without your permission.

Thank goodness I made a good decision when I discovered the first BEANSTALK. I have interviewed many people who chose DENIAL as an OPTION which prolonged the agony until breaking point arrived. I've interviewed people where ISOLATION was the OPTION they chose. They just built more and more walls around themselves to protect them but then realised how that in itself had negative repercussions.

NEGATIVE ATTITUDE: Is a disposition, feeling, or manner that is not constructive, cooperative or optimistic. Synonyms: pessimistic, defeatist, cynical, bleak, dismissive, damaging, detrimental.

**POSITIVE ATTITUDE: Having a good effect;
favourable; marked by optimism.
Synonyms: constructive, practical, useful,
productive, beneficial, hopeful, encouraging**

One of my favourite words that I use often in my own MIND
GARDEN is CONSTRUCTIVE.

**CONSTRUCTIVE: Having or intended to have a
useful or beneficial purpose.
Synonyms: productive, practical, worthwhile, effective**

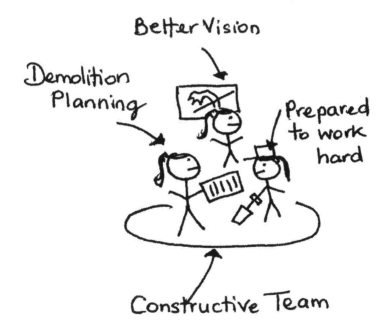

When dealing with BEANSTALKS I choose to have a
CONSTRUCTIVE ATTITUDE. I often have a positive attitude
in life but it is not always realistic to be happy and positive

when dealing with the difficult and strugglesome emotions that DEMOLITION can bring. It is far healthier for me to expect myself to be CONSTRUCTIVE. So, I get the hard hat out.

I also get the TEAM involved and make a united plan of campaign. There is so much SELF-KNOWLEDGE to be acquired from studying your BEANSTALKS (if you have them) and so much SELF-CONFIDENCE to be gained from digging them up and using them in your COMPOST BIN to then NOURISH your SOIL. The freedom, happiness and lighter feelings are worth every effort you put in. I used to let my BEANSTALKS define my garden... now I say:

"I don't think so you pesty BEANSTALK. Watch out! I've got a good axe and a very effective swing."

Empowerment is a wonderful thing.

4. WEEDS

Common Mind Garden Weeds

- Environment
- Lack of Self-Discipline
- Lack of Purpose
- Lack of Self-Control
- Lack of Ambition
- Overcaution
- Insufficient Education
- Ill Health
- Procrastination
- Lack of Persistence
- Wrong selection of partner
- Fear
- Indiscriminate Spending
- Debt

WEED: A wild plant growing where it is not wanted
and in competition with cultivated plants.
Synonyms: I'm not going to lie, the only synonym for
weed was Marijuana! So we'll move on!

I remember my garden full of weeds. They seemed to strangle any cultivated plants I was trying to grow. I mean, how many unintentional weeds can one girl possibly grow?

I mentioned previously about WEEDS growing as a direct result of BEANSTALKS but there are other types of WEEDS which may not be rooted in the past. These may come from bad habits that have formed over time due to lack of GARDEN DESIGN or MANAGEMENT. They may also grow from a current situation or simply NEGLECTING to look after the garden on a regular basis. WEEDS can grow quickly if left unchecked and although some may be easy to pull out and discard, others may be more stubborn and keep returning, which can be irritating and demoralising. WEEDS can also appear in the form of FEARS which are human nature but if left to grow wild, can become out of hand.

I have been a student of Napoleon Hill's "Think and Grow Rich" for the last seven years. I made 48 pages of A4 notes on it which I refer to often. The title put me off for a long time because money wasn't my aim but how wrong could I have been to judge the title. There is a definite slant towards the accumulation of money but I gained far more knowledge about FEARS and self-imposed restrictions (another variety of WEED) than in any other book. It was painstaking to write down the reasons why things may fail to grow in my garden successfully. Many of them I associate as WEEDS. Being aware of them can help to look objectively at your own garden to ASSESS which ones may be causing distress in your own life. Education really is power. When you KNOW the WEEDS and you find out they are not CONSTRUCTIVE, then it is the first step to WEED REMOVAL, or in other words WEEDING.

I also learned a lot about WEEDS from Jim Rohn. A few common and very damaging weeds are:

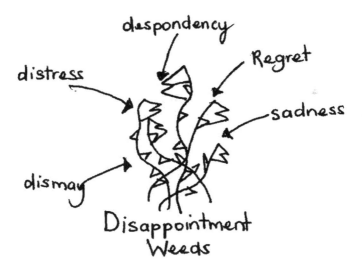

DISAPPOINTMENT: Sadness or displeasure caused by the non-fulfilment of one's hopes or expectations. Synonyms: regret, dismay, despondency, distress

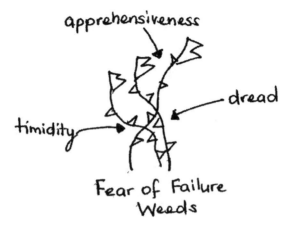

apprehensiveness

dread

timidity

Fear of Failure
Weeds

FEAR OF FAILURE: Also known as 'atychiphobia'
is when we allow that fear to stop us doing the things that
can move us forward to achieve our goals.
Synonyms: apprehensiveness, dread, timidity

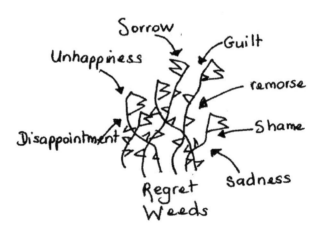

Sorrow

Guilt

Unhappiness

remorse

Shame

Disappointment

Sadness

Regret
Weeds

REGRET: A feeling of sadness, repentance or
disappointment over an occurrence or something that one
has done or failed to do.
Synonyms: remorse, sorrow, guilt, shame

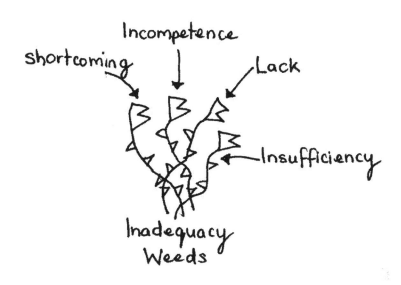

INADEQUACY: Lack of the quantity or quality required.
Synonyms: insufficiency, lack, shortcoming

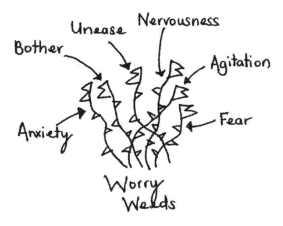

WORRY: The state of being anxious and troubled over actual or potential problems.
Synonyms: anxiety, bother, unease, nervousness, agitation, fear

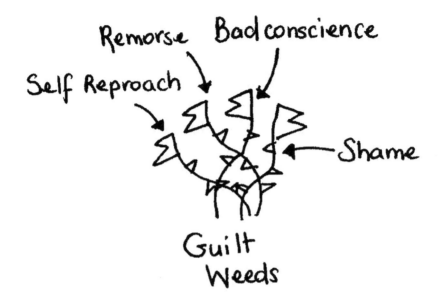

Remorse Bad conscience

Self Reproach

Shame

Guilt

Weeds

GUILT: A feeling of having committed wrong or failed in an obligation.
Synonyms: self-reproach, a bad conscience, remorse, shame

Being aware of my WEEDS was one thing. Getting rid of them and preventing their return has been on ongoing process that enhances my MIND GARDEN so much. It would be unrealistic to say I was always WEED FREE but because I garden regularly it isn't often that I find myself deeply entangled.

For me, the main aim is to turn the WEED upside down and unearth it by learning about it, analysing it and studying how I could plant the complete opposite of that WEED and cultivate a beautiful flower instead. This usually requires some research, time and education. I also use the WISDOM HAT and sit by the issue to see whether it is something that I can or cannot change. The Serenity Prayer is very useful:

"Please grant me the SERENITY to ACCEPT the things I cannot change, COURAGE to CHANGE the things I can and WISDOM to know the difference

My MANAGER is now in charge of WEED MANAGEMENT. It is an essential role. As with any real life garden, if WEEDING is done regularly it is far less time consuming and daunting than if it's left a few weeks/months/years. My advice would be REGULAR CHECKS followed by an ACTION plan to remove them.

In my experience:
COMPETENCE leads to CONFIDENCE.

GROWTH LABORATORY EXPERIMENT:
Assessing Weeds

STEP 1: FIND OUT WHERE THE WEEDS ARE
With the help of the LAWN OF LIFE (Next Chapter)
find out where the WEEDS are.

STEP 2: NAME THE WEEDS
Label the WEEDS and ASSESS their ROOTS

STEP 3: CREATE A PLAN OF ACTION
Decide on a plan to remove them if possible.

STEP 4: POSITIVE NOURISHMENT
Replace the WEED with POSITIVE
NOURISHMENT to the SOIL

STEP 5: REPEAT REGULARLY
Schedule in a regular WEED check.

As you become able to transform the WEEDS into positives, your inner confidence will start to feel natural in your foundations. That's when things can really start to grow for the better.

5. THE LAWN OF LIFE

Family /Friends /Connect
Relationship / Intimacy
Health and Well Being
Work / Retirement
Money and Finances
Personal Growth
Fun and Adventures
Physical Environment
Contribution
Vision for the Future

The LAWN OF LIFE is my Life Assessment Tool. It is for assessing how I feel about everything that's going on in areas of importance to me. I first completed a tool like this after reading 'How to be Brilliant' by Michael Heppell. In his book he called it the Wheel of Life. I have tweaked it for the Thinklesticks MIND GARDEN to fit with the analogy.

The LAWN is divided into 10 strips:

1. Family / Friends / Connections
2. Relationship / Intimacy
3. Health and Well Being
4. Career/Work or Retirement
5. Money and Finances
6. Personal Growth
7. Fun and Adventures
8. Physical Environment
9. Contribution
10. Vision for the Future

When you look at a beautiful LAWN in real life, it is well tended to, it's watered and cut regularly so it doesn't get too unmanageable, weeds are removed by hand or with weed killer, new grass seeds are sprinkled over barren areas and care is taken not to carelessly trample on it.

If one or more strips or areas of a lawn look dry, you notice them. In fact it can often spoil the entire look of the lawn and focus is drawn to the irritation of those areas rather than the lush green parts that are thriving. If weeds overtake one area they can quickly spread to others.

As mentioned previously in the GARDEN EMPLOYMENT chapter, I now employ a LAWN SPECIALIST, who does regular checks on the LAWN OF LIFE to make sure it's looking as healthy and lush as possible. Various things can affect the LAWN and so it's important to know why it's looking the way it is and be proactive in helping it thrive rather than leaving it too long and having to rescue it from its sorry state.

I think there are a few main causes of LAWN DAMAGE that I've experienced:

SOIL: damage in the roots (SELF ESTEEM)
WEED: damage from ongoing issues
NEGLECT: not enough intentional watering
OVERWATERING: in one or more areas
SEASONS: fluctuating external events

The great thing about assessing the LAWN OF LIFE is that I've found that it can make me see where my areas of strength lie. Sometimes I can be feeling a bit low but when I see an overview of things I realise that it might only be a few strips of grass that need a bit of work to regain a nice LAWN.

HOW TO ASSESS THE LAWN OF LIFE

1. Look at each strip of the LAWN and rate it from 0-10 depending on how you feel about it in general. Don't take too long on your answers.

2. Add up your total score out of 100.

3. This is your GARDEN SNAPSHOT for the day.

4. Take this SNAPSHOT to the GROWTH LAB

5. Examine the LOWEST numbers and see if you can establish the cause of it (e.g. Is it not watered regularly, has an event happened, is there a weed infestation?)

6. Take a few steps each week to deal with the findings.

7. Aim to gradually increase the numbers with POSITIVE ACTION.

8. If your numbers are higher, still take a look at the lowest numbers and see what steps can be taken to improve even more.

9. Repeat LAWN MANAGEMENT regularly as early prevention is easier than a RESCUE MISSION.

10. As your overall LAWN of LIFE numbers improve you will find it increasingly enjoyable to sit and smile at it.

I take my LAWN numbers and try to improve a couple of areas by one point at a time. It helps to guide me on how to feel better. I found that it was usually the FUN and ADVENTURE areas which would be low when I was really busy with everyday life. If that was the case, I would sit and think about something I'd like to do and plan it with a friend. Even having one or two adventures to look forward to was enough to up my numbers from a 4 to a 5. The power of even the tiniest positive, intentional shift to improve the LAWN can be inspiring. I recommend it!

6. THE GREENHOUSE

GREENHOUSE: A building with a roof and sides made of glass or other transparent material, used for growing plants that need warmth and protection.
Synonyms: hothouse, nursery, potting shed

Ah, the GREENHOUSE. I cannot help but smile when I write this chapter. I mentioned previously in the GARDEN EMPLOYMENT section that I have a GREENHOUSE SPECIALIST role which is very important to me. When my garden was left to its own devices it was a mess. This didn't mean that there weren't things that could grow which were good and enjoyable, it just meant it was very much pot luck if that happened and it was usually from someone else planting the seed of suggestion in my mind.

In 2011, that all changed. In the year when I took my PERSONAL DEVELOPMENT on as a challenge, I studied SUCCESS. I wanted to improve life for my family and myself and so I decided that a sensible way to do this would be to look at how other people had become successful. I started to read. I became fascinated. I could see patterns. There was a lot of information about GOAL SETTING and ACHIEVING GOALS which led to SUCCESS. I also understood that SUCCESS means different things to different people and I started to think about what it meant to me. How would I know if I was successful? Would it be the bottom line of my bank account? Or would it be how many times I felt joy in a day? What would success look like in different areas of the LAWN OF LIFE? Why did I want to be successful?

I think the truthful answer was that I wanted life to feel better. The struggles had been difficult. I'd managed so far but I just had a niggling feeling that things could be better, that I had more to give and the quality of our lives could be improved.

I decided to write a statement to help me aim for my own kind of success. It took a long time to do but it was an excellent guiding exercise in terms of helping me to grow an internal garden which reflects these words.

"I want to live a life of love and connection, generosity and joy, fun and freedom, abundance and adventure, happiness and good health, kindness and compassion, excitement and expansion, growth and humility. I want to always be digging at my potential and encourage others to dig at theirs. I want to do what I love and love what I do. I want to honour the struggles and learn the lessons. I want to have a mind that works for me and not against me. I want to create a life I love. That will be success. Every single day I will be grateful that I am being given the opportunity to give it my best shot in the hope that I will be of great service to the world around me." Joanna Louise Wright, 2011.

I began to read the statement often. It was in the back of my journal. Every time I started a new journal I would rewrite it at the back. It had been a powerful exercise and I recommend it. The DESIGNER had been responsible for sitting down and thinking about what I wanted.

I read a lot about how you can GROW through setting a GOAL that feels bigger than you. Something that feels exciting and challenging. So I decided to do an experiment in the GROWTH LAB.

GROWTH LABORATORY EXPERIMENT:
Can you GROW to the size of a GOAL?

STEP 1: PURCHASE A GREENHOUSE
Decide whether it is big, small or just right.

STEP 2: DECIDE ON A DREAM SEED
Choose a dream to experiment with.

STEP 3: PLANT THE DREAM SEED
Start the process with one small step.

STEP 4: LEARN TO NURTURE IT
Pay it regular attention, daily if possible.

STEP 5: DEVELOP THE SKILLS
Develop the skill necessary to support the growth of the DREAM SEED.

STEP 6: PROTECT FROM NEGATIVITY
Protect the DREAM SEED from negative inside and outside influences.

STEP 7: BE PATIENT
Learn to persist and be patient. (Tricky!)

STEP 8: SEEDLINGS OF HOPE
If a SEEDLING OF HOPE sprouts up, get very excited!

STEP 9: REPLANT
Look after the SEEDLING and EPLANT in a bigger pot with even more POSITIVITY and RESEARCH

STEP 10: PLANT IN MAIN GARDEN
When the DREAM SEED has grown into a healthy and flourishing plant/flower make a plan to replant in the MAIN GARDEN to share with others but still protect from NEGATIVITY

STEP 11: REALLY ENJOY IT
Enjoy the FLOURISHING DREAM FLOWER and be proud of the process and all you have learned along the way.

STEP 12: ANALYSE
If the DREAM SEED doesn't grow, analyse carefully why, and then choose another SEED to try.

Having interviewed many people about their own MIND GARDENS, it became apparent that many did not own a GREENHOUSE. When I delved deeper it seemed to link with the fact that lots of people suffer from a FEAR OF FAILURE. They might desperately want to live a life they love, or achieve a long held dream and develop a gift or talent but, for whatever reason, they have been put off doing this.

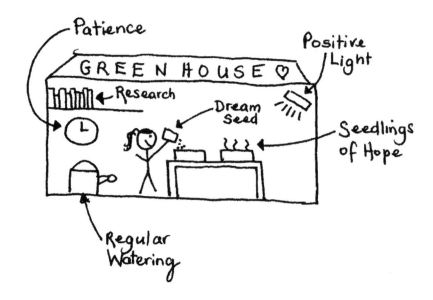

I can only go on the feelings that I had earlier in life but I know that a lot of the things I tried to plant just didn't work out, or other people had spoiled, or I didn't have the skills to make it a success. Those failures, and they were failures, were very damaging to my WORKER's morale and my DESIGNER's dreams. The saying "Try and try again" used to annoy me because actually, when you've tried and tried again and not got the results you were hoping for, it can be very demoralising. It can also lead to a lot of inner pain that you might try and brush off on the surface but internally it can quickly turn into WEEDS of DOUBT, FEAR and INSECURITY. Often, we are very closely attached to our dreams and goals. If they don't work out, it is difficult to separate ourselves from the failure and disappointment. We become the failure, rather than seeing the situations as isolated incidents. Those WEEDS are the enemy of CONFIDENCE and COURAGE.

Things started to change when I altered my PERCEPTION of aiming for a goal.

SUCCESS: The accomplishment of a desired aim or purpose.
Synonyms: favourable outcome, victory, triumph

So in 2012, I decided to put all the reading to the test. I'd listened to countless hours of Personal Development speakers, read numerous books about goal setting and the benefits of thinking about what you want, making a plan and going for it. I enjoyed the GROWTH LABORATORY experiments. Putting the theories to the test seemed to take the pressure off me personally. I was, in fact, just trialling out whether the wisdom worked for me, rather than relying on my own confidence. I suppose it was easier to follow guidelines and proven paths than just use guesswork, like I had in the past.

Around the same time, I read an article in 'PSYCHOLOGIES' magazine. It was saying that if you put 30 minutes a day to moving your dream forward you can achieve anything.

So I made the decision that the DREAM SEED I would plant in my brand new GREENHOUSE would be:

TO WRITE A NOVEL and TO HAVE THE BOOK ON MY SHELF.

SCEPTICAL: Not easily convinced; having doubts or reservations.
Synonyms: dubious, doubtful, cynical

The amazing thing was that I didn't believe for one minute that I could do it. The advice said:

"If you believe it, you can achieve it."
"Imagine you have already achieved the goal."
"Visualise yourself in possession of your goal."

Mmm. I was very bad at this. I couldn't picture myself as an Author because it was an absolute pipe dream. So far away from who I was. I had managed to work out that it was something I would love to do. My DESIGNER had encouraged me to get a GREENHOUSE and give it a go. My MANAGER was behind the idea and scheduled in 30 minutes a day. My WORKER, though, was not convinced in any way that it was going to happen. I captured those early doubts in my journals.

"I have no idea what I am doing but I'm going to follow the plan." Joanna Louise Wright 2012.

I soon realised that my WORKER was in need of help with the role of the GREENHOUSE SPECIALIST. The WORKER's negativity was going to be harmful to the DREAM SEED. I decided that the GREENHOUSE SPECIALIST needed to be focused on the possible SUCCESS of growing the dream rather than its certain failure. Positivity was a key factor in all of the wisdom.

And so it began.

30 Minutes a day.

Every day.

I could never have imagined how much I was to learn about myself during the process. I had not grasped the full meaning of GROWING into the person that can achieve a big dream. Looking back on it now I have evaluated the amazing benefits and outcomes of planting the DREAM SEED in the GREENHOUSE and the incredible adventure it took me on.

The wonderful thing about having a GREENHOUSE is that you don't have to wait for the perfect time to plant something. You are not trying to plant the DREAM SEED in your main MIND GARDEN, so you can be working on growing a little seedling in the GREENHOUSE at the same time as you are doing some GARDEN CLEARANCE of WEEDS and BEANSTALKS or NOURISHING the SOIL. When you have a GREENHOUSE it can add a bit of welcome distraction, excitement, hope and positivity. Knowing you are working on a future project which is safe from damage from the main garden can be a huge breath of fresh air…every single day.

I've also learned a lot about the SEEDS that fail to grow, for whatever reason. The GREENHOUSE is the prime location for trialling things out before transferring into the MAIN GARDEN. I've often had flashes of inspiration, which I've planted as an IDEA SEED but as I've gone through the process of research, or even to the next stage of replanting, I've found that it's just not bringing to my garden what I thought it would. I am never afraid to then put it in the COMPOST BIN. The whole process would still have taught me a lot, but I wholeheartedly believe that you should only invest your time in the things that are potentially going to bring you the most joy.

"Your mind is like a garden - if you do not deliberately plant flowers and tend to them carefully, weeds will grow without any encouragement at all." - Brian Tracy.

The GREENHOUSE enables me to GROW the things I DREAM of and develop my skills, knowledge, character and personality at the same time. The things I grow also benefit the world around me. It is never selfish to spend time in your

GREENHOUSE. It is one of the best things you can do for the world. The world needs the things that only you can create with your unique set of skills, talents and gifts.

After Self-Publishing 'Benchmark', I received so many emails and messages from people who were inspired by the story. This was a complete shock to me. I had not been expecting my words to touch so many people. It made me realise the importance of sharing the gifts of your SOIL. You never know when your GROWTH will help someone else's.

7. GARDEN BORDERS

BORDER: Form an edge, along or beside.
Synonyms: surround, edge, neighbour

In MIND GARDEN terms, BORDERS represent a few things and can be such a complex area. This has been arguably the hardest part of the garden to manage because ultimately, it involves other people. Here are a few of the things I will cover in GARDEN BORDERS:

Communication
Relationships
Friendships
Sharing
Personality
Attitude
Perception
Perspective
Boundaries
Common ground
Vulnerability
Security

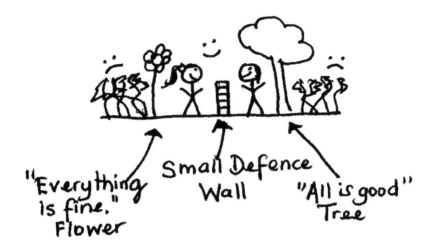

"Everything is fine." Flower   Small Defence Wall   "All is good" Tree

The reason I first became fascinated about this topic was because when I had been suffering my internal breakdown and my lowest times, I had been able to 'keep up a front'. In other words I put on a facade.

FACADE: The front, or outside of something. The other meaning has to do with people who are hiding something. In both cases, the facade could be deceiving. A person putting on a facade means the face they're showing to the world doesn't match how they're feeling.
Synonyms: false display, illusion, pretence.

This was very damaging at the time because I would internally berate myself for being false. If someone asked how I was, I would reply cheerfully, "Good thanks, you?" when internally I was far from good. That false response triggered nasty little voices to appear from inside:

"You are so fake."

"I need to get away from here before I'm found out."

The worst consequence of that response was that I had shut

down any chance of offloading some of the pain and sharing it. I had put up a wall so the person couldn't see what a tangled mess my inner garden was. The wall created a barrier to stop any effective, authentic communication and the ultimate result, I was alone.

Yet, I wasn't deliberately misleading or deceiving people. At the time, it felt as if I was protecting them from having to be a part of the mess I'd made of myself. I suppose I was also ashamed and confused. I didn't understand how I was feeling. To try and explain it seemed too overwhelming. A quick "I'm fine" always seemed like the easier option. In MIND GARDEN terms, I created GARDEN BORDERS to explain and investigate how our INNER GARDENS differ from the GARDEN BORDERS we present to the rest of the world. I truly believe this is a vital part of humanity that we are getting so wrong. I certainly got it wrong at the time when I needed authentic human connection more than anything. After interviewing my first 50 people, I realised that many of them related to my description of feeling as if they are spending a lot of time on their BORDERS, fearing judgement, and that their inner gardens told a very different story from what they were representing to the world. Not everyone had terribly entangled gardens like mine but many needed a lot of work and it felt overwhelming, yet I would never, ever have realised that from the first "Hi, how are you?" surface chat.

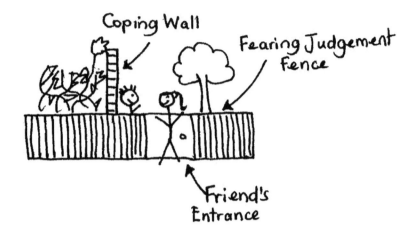

I was amazed at how talking through the Thinklesticks MIND GARDEN analogy people were able to open up to me very quickly, in general terms, how the internal experience of their world felt and also how they thought others perceived their experience to be. When there was a clear difference between these two things I immediately sensed pain, hurt, stress, discomfort, struggle and vulnerability. I was being let into the internal gardens where not many people, if any, were allowed. Some people said they'd never told ANYONE some of the things that were unearthed by me interviewing them and it was clearly a relief to finally not be alone with those issues and to realise there may be things they could do to make changes. Every time I came away from an interview, I just had more determination to get Thinklesticks MIND GARDEN published and out there. I feel more passionately about GARDEN BORDERS now that I know, for sure, that I was not an isolated case. Depression, anxiety, stress, addiction, health problems and a huge amount of internal, unknown suffering is going on silently all around us. I have a personal mission to make that change. In whatever way I can. Talking about the real, inner battles we all have as humans can connect us on deep, fulfilling levels and there really should be no need for loneliness and isolation if we are all playing our parts.

It's not all doom and gloom on the BORDER front though. A lot of joy and positive connections can be created and I'm very happy to say that I have, in the most part, been able to cultivate authentic borders and common ground with an ever expanding, wonderful network of people. I've had to learn those skills and practise them to be able to communicate effectively, to help myself and others. This has meant overcoming FEARS and ANXIETIES but it's liberating when you do. When you are comfortable to let your true self out into the open to communicate with other people authentically, you realise you don't have to spend so much time tidying up the borders for other people's benefit, leaving more time to actually enjoy interactions.

Studying COMMUNICATION was very interesting. It is such a vast subject and one that I would advise everyone to delve into, especially if you lack confidence in social situations. One of the most important things I learned, which helped with my anxiety of being judged, was to completely flip that idea on its head. Instead of going into a room thinking:

"I bet everyone will look at me and think I'm ugly." WEED from school (which is now completely dug out of my garden!)

I trained myself to take the limelight off myself internally and think:

"I wonder what I can learn about the people in this room."

So I went to the GARDEN BORDER with a completely different agenda. I only had to do this once to realise how powerful it was. I came away from the interaction having learned something interesting. It had been a positive encounter and rapport had taken place with no inner turmoil on my part. Rather than the alternative of second guessing every look the people were giving me, internally backing up my theory that they thought I was ugly, hence feeling worse after the interaction and feeding the WEED.

COMMON GROUND: A basis of mutual interest or agreement.
Synonyms: mutual understanding, commonalities, mutuality

Another piece of wisdom I live by every day is reminding myself that everyone is facing their own battle. In this analogy that means that you never know what someone's internal garden feels like to them, unless, you ask. Not in a nosey, gossiping way, but in a caring, authentic way. Having studied BORDERS and COMMUNICATION in such depth, I really do know the value that a positive interaction can have and how damaging a negative one can be.

Also, the more you work on your own garden, SOIL, WEEDS, BEANSTALKS, GREENHOUSE and GARDEN EMPLOYMENT, the more you can relate to other people's emotions and situations and be as compassionate as possible.

Finding COMMON GROUND is the most effective way to create meaningful connections, friendships and relationships. When I meet any new person, I approach them with openness. They are a fellow human. That is our COMMON GROUND. I do not look for the differences. I look for similarities. Once the COMMON GROUND has been firmly established it is then fascinating to explore the differences too and learn about their gardens.

I find it useful to focus on thinking about my BORDERS every so often. Sometimes habits can form, or unconscious choices depending on what mood you are in, can affect how you naturally greet people. Bearing in mind how important our interactions can be with other people, if you start off frosty, behind a spiky bush just in case that person is out to hurt you, the chances are they'll spot the spikes in the bush straight away and stay clear. Who knows how much that person had to give or how much they might have needed a friendly face. The bush got in the way. Now you'll never know.

I read something somewhere that a simple "Hello" to a stranger (obviously assessing any obvious safety concerns) can be a wonderful thing and can lead to a fulfilling human connection. It was saying that this can take courage as you risk the person rejecting you by ignoring you completely, but that if you saw it as an experiment, you wouldn't take it so personally. I remember the first time I tried this out. I was at the supermarket, in the cat food aisle. There was an elderly man next to me trying to decide what type to buy. I said "There's too much choice isn't there?" I felt a bit weird starting up the conversation but he laughed, smiled and started a story about his cat. He seemed so happy to have had a chit-chat, he wished me a good day and off I went. The joy of the simple connection was surprising to me. I felt we had been significant to each other in a small way and it made me smile. Needless to say, I now love having more open BORDERS. It's changed my experience of the world for the better.

I am much happier now that I have friendly, open BORDERS after conquering my fear of judgment. It caused a lot of inner turmoil and I brought most of it on myself by imagining what people must be thinking when in truth, what did it really matter what they thought? So many wasted opportunities because I put a wall up, or a high fence, or a border of high trees to protect myself from possible hurt. The thing is, when you have those protective barriers, they might keep the negative from coming in but they also prevent the best things entering.

I made a conscious decision to become a person who would be friendly, open, approachable and kind at my BORDER. That does not mean I am vulnerable to people taking advantage of that. If someone comes at me with a vicious thorn or a poisonous plant I will immediately get my 24 hour Security Team in to sort it out. I won't let nastiness in to my garden. I don't expect nastiness to ever be at my

BORDER so I do not place barriers up just in case. One bad experience does not make me spoil the BORDER for the next 100 people who walk towards me. If I didn't look after my BORDERS regularly, that might not be the case.

I've made the focus of this Thinklesticks book PERSONAL journeys and MIND GARDENS as individual things. I am well aware, though, that SHARED GARDENS are very important to cultivate and look after too. I could write a whole book about SHARED GARDENS, and no doubt I will one day, but I will briefly describe my thoughts here.

Relationships, I believe, are created on COMMON GROUND. It is there that things can be grown together, either as an intimate relationship, children, family or friendship. Each person brings their own SOIL and, to some extent, WEEDS with them from their own gardens. This means that COMMON GROUND areas have the potential to be complex. Often, a lot of time is spent in COMMON GROUND areas and sometimes the individual gardens get left behind. If that is the case, eventually they will become overgrown and affect the COMMON GROUND area too. That is why I believe that everyone is responsible for their own personal gardens and time should be spent in there as well as in COMMON GROUND. I could definitely write 20,000 words on this subject but I've got a deadline to meet so I'll leave that for another day!

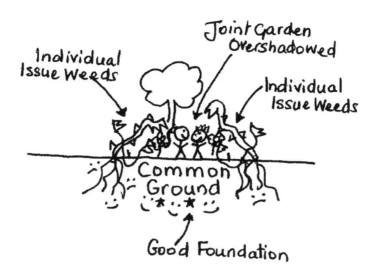

FUN: Enjoyment, amusement or light-hearted pleasure."
Synonyms: pleasure, leisure, great time

Now this is a word that I love. Fun. I am very happy to say that in my MIND GARDEN I now have multiple PLAYGROUNDS on COMMON GROUND with various groups of friends and family. In other words, happy playful places where memories are made. I think PLAYGROUNDS are essential for a fulfilling garden otherwise too much time can be spent working. I do work hard in my job and on myself but I also play almost as much. Knowing I've done the work lets me really enjoy the play with no feelings of guilt that I should be doing something else. I've interviewed people who have said that they often spend too much time in the PLAYGROUND and put off doing the work in the main garden. This eventually leads to a giant mess that they have to return to. For me, the PLAYGROUND is a place where I go to reward myself for getting the work done. I am very lucky to have such brilliant friends and family to spend time with. Life can be challenging but a bit of fun can be exactly what your WORKER needs to feel revitalised.

8. SEASONS AND STORMS

Jim Rohn introduced me to the idea that we tend to go through seasons. I certainly agree that I can apply that analogy to my own life. It also fits perfectly into my MIND GARDEN work.

Summer: Bright, fun, happy
Autumn: Change, transition, unsettled
Winter: Cold, bleak, dark
Spring: Hopeful, budding, lighter

It helps me greatly to know which season it feels like in my internal world. I have developed tactics, tools, strategies and support systems for each season to help get the most out of them. Every single day varies, yet seasons are an overall mood. A break up, loss of a loved one, ill health, a crisis or traumatic event may cause a period of change and uncertainty. I have learned to try not to fight the seasons. In Autumn and Winter I accept that things are more naturally difficult. Yet MIND GARDENING is always useful in any season. Knowing and accepting that I am in a Winter can be incredibly comforting especially if I am able to put things into place to help me through that bleaker time. Reaching out to friends to talk by the fire. Looking after myself to a high standard with good food and lots of rest in front of a feel good film. Plenty of sifting to make sure I am setting the garden up for Spring in the best possible way.

"The ending of a job or relationship may appear as the darkest night but it is merely the Winter season - the time of renewal and rebirth that precedes the new planting - the beginning of the next great cycle." - Jonathan Lockwood Huie

I allow myself those Autumns and Winters yet I keep my eyes and mind firmly on the next Spring and Summer. I still do whatever work I can in those more difficult seasons so that when the lighter months do arrive, there is more chance that the blooms will be extra special. Being aware and conscious about being in Spring and Summer makes me appreciate them all the more. When things are going well, I make the most of those times.

Knowing that each season will pass brings comfort. If it's been a long Winter, make plans for the Spring. It it's been an amazing Summer, take time to make Snapshots to look back on. If it's an unsettling Autumn, know that sometimes the best things come from the transitions of life. If it's a hopeful Spring, enjoy every new bud opening with a grateful heart.

What season are you in right now? It's a very useful question.

I've experienced a few STORMS in my life. Events that caused destruction on a mass scale, bringing a complete halt to all normal gardening work. When you are in a STORM you know about it. These are often completely unexpected events and you have little or no control over them. This may coincide with an Autumn or Winter or maybe just arrive completely out of the blue. The worst STORM I encountered was when my youngest son had a bicycle accident and lacerated his liver. We lived in hospital for 7 weeks and he had 7 operations. During STORM season it can be incredibly stressful. I now have part-time EMERGENCY SERVICES as roles in my MIND GARDEN for those extremely difficult times. I do still believe that strategies can be put in place to support my mind at this time. Asking for help, meditation, taking things hour by hour. The brain and body are on RED ALERT at these times so it's important to try to regain control as quickly as possible and make a plan for STRESS MANAGEMENT. Once the STORM has passed and recovery has taken place, I get back to ASSESSING and ADDRESSING the damage as soon as possible.

9. PATIO OF INNER PEACE

Now, I know I've talked a lot about the work I put into my MIND GARDEN but now for the happiest chapter of them all. I believe, with all of me, that the more work you put in to your MIND GARDEN; the daily MANAGEMENT, the WEEDING, the digging up of damaging long standing BEANSTALKS, the tending to the LAWN OF LIFE, the development of healthy BORDERS and the ongoing training of the GARDEN EMPLOYMENT TEAM, the more joy, happiness and peace you feel when you sit back on the PATIO and observe the view. When you can look up and see the progress, where there was once a massive overgrowth strangling the beauty of life, you now see gorgeous landscaped areas which you designed and grew from tiny seeds, huge waves of fulfilment, pride and fondness fill your heart. As long as I am alive, there will always be garden issues and jobs to do. Like nature, life stops for no one. Whereas, in the past, my fear of the next problem popping up was a constant low level anxiety, now with the structure of my MIND GARDEN and all the tools I have in place, I do not fear problems. I'd be lying if I said I welcome them into my garden but if they arise, I'm on it and I will find a way to process it to get the best outcome for my garden to thrive. When I glance over to my greenhouse, excitement and enthusiasm bubble up inside me as I know the next dreams are either being planted, tended to or about to be replanted into the main garden to flourish. Every successful area of the garden tells a story of personal growth, that only I know the true extent of. The hours I've spent training in resilience, in goal setting, in overcoming fears, in time management and when I sit back, on my PATIO, I love what I see.

So, no matter what your MIND GARDEN feels like today, I encourage you to get your garden gloves and start on a plan for development. When your garden thrives it's amazing how much it helps, not only you but your neighbouring gardens and the world around you.

I hope one day I'll get to take a walk around your mind garden. Until then…

Dig deep and never underestimate the power of a cultivated mind.

Patio of Inner Peace

TESTIMONIALS
FROM THE THINKLESTICKS
MIND GARDEN INTERVIEWS

"Absolutely loved my mind garden interview. It was like free therapy. I instantly connected with the super effective garden analogy. My garden is now spectacular as a result of our interview and I have the best garden management team to keep any weeds out. What an amazing way to address deeper issues and make positive life changes. Inspirational doodles plus relatable analogies are a winning formula. The world needs Thinklesticks" - Keisha

"The Mind Garden is a clever & simple concept that everyone can & should learn to use. It offers a great set of tools to help organise and change your mindset to be positive & manageable. After my initial interview I used The Mind Garden analogy of 'chopping down my beanstalk ' ...powerful stuff!" - Tina

When Jo asked me if I would be willing to take part in an interview as part of her research for her new book I was only too happy to help. Jo is such a lovely person and I had so enjoyed her first foray into publishing, "Benchmark". Little did I realise that her clever interviewing skills would bring out emotions in me that I thought were long-buried. So, far from me helping Jo, she helped me in so many ways. I'm sure this new book will do the same for all who read it." - Beverley

"I underwent a Mind Garden interview with Joanna earlier this year. Not only is Joanna really open and **friendly**, which puts you at ease, the interview is cleverly structured around something all of us can relate to. It makes understanding your emotions, their causes and how to manage them so much simpler. The fact Joanna has included the Thinklesticks doodles as a visual element makes the Mind Garden even more accessible - even for someone like me, who isn't usually a visual person. A fantastic way of getting more people to recognise and learn to manage their emotions as opposed to the other way round. Genius in fact! I'd highly recommend!" - Tanya

"When you live a life going through the motions every single day and start to neglect the hedges, the lawn and most importantly the soil you begin to slowly start losing control. You see, I always thought I was living in the Garden of Eden, everybody else's perception of paradise because that's what society wanted for me, it was what my parents wanted for me. Was it what I wanted for me? Maybe? Maybe at the time? Sitting down with Joanna and watching my garden unfold right In front of my eyes hit me like a hail storm! I walked away knowing exactly what I needed to do and only I could be the gardener of my own garden. My life has literally taken a massive turn since but I am a work in progress and I cannot wait to tell you all about my new garden of Eden, the garden I am going to invest all my time in from now on." - Marlene

"I've found gardening therapeutic. It wasn't until I met with Joanna and started talking about Thinklesticks that I realised the metaphorical significance of gardening in terms of sorting through the thought process. I like the simplicity of the ideas yet very effective and refreshing. I'd recommend the mind garden exercises for anyone who wants to get more insight into how they think and process life experience." - Winsa

"I think the idea of a mind garden is so refreshing because it's such a different way to talk about Mental Health. The idea is simple, user friendly and even though it seems light hearted it includes lots of elements including the darker stuff that is hard to talk about. The different parts of the garden and the people in it break down different areas of life and explain what someone needs to have good mental health without being preaching or judgemental. The garden is an easy to follow instruction manual for when difficult times strike and offers a way out. The idea can also be adapted for each individual and maybe a pleasant place to go when it is completed and maintained. - Ellen

"The Mind Garden provided a very simple analogy to explain the complexities of the mind. It made perfect sense to me to think of my mind as a garden; as it is a tangled web built up of life experiences which lead to seeds being sown and plants that I had started growing. As I began to discuss and compare my experiences to a garden many things made sense and I was able to organise my understanding of my own thoughts, feelings and experiences that have been both negative and positive throughout my life. My garden was beautiful, green and full of life; however, there were still some weeds that required tending to now and then to keep in check. At the time of my interview my life was going through some challenges and my attitude towards people in general had changed. I realised that the fence to my garden was low enough to wave over and invite friends in, but high enough to not let certain people in. Later on, in the year I did find myself revisiting my garden and I realised that it could be changed; the fence could be lowered and some of those weeds could be eradicated over time."- Justin

"I met with Joanna whilst in a vulnerable state and after an hour or so with her she helped me visualise and clear some of the tangle in my head and I walked away somehow lighter and with a more positive state of mind."- Katrina

A massive thank you to everyone who has taken part in a Mind Garden Interview. Your time, insight and openness are priceless to me. I will be continuing my Research Project for many years to come.

For more Thinklesticks inspiration please join the Social Media Community on Facebook, Instagram, Twitter and Pinterest.

Coming Soon
www.thinklesticks.com

Online Courses
www.thinklesticksacademy.com

ABOUT THE AUTHOR

Joanna Louise Wright is an emotive writer with a personal passion for self-development which weaves into all of her work, touching the hearts and minds of her readers. Born in London and now living in Reading, England. She Self Published her first novel 'Benchmark' in July 2015 which is available on Amazon.

Printed in Great Britain
by Amazon